A Time for Embracing

A Time for Embracing

Reclaiming Reconciliation

Julia Upton, R.S.M.

A Liturgical Press Book

THE LITURGICAL PRESS
Collegeville, Minnesota

Quotations from the documents of Vatican II are taken from *Vatican Council II: The Basic Sixteen Documents*, ed. Austin Flannery, O.P. (North-port, N.Y.: Costello Publishing Co., 1996), a completely revised translation in inclusive language.

Quotations from the Rite of Penance (RP) are taken from *The Rites of the Catholic Church*, Vol. 2, prepared by the International Commission on English in the Liturgy (Collegeville, Minn.: The Liturgical Press, 1991).

The Scripture quotations are from the New Revised Standard Version Bible, Catholic edition, © 1989 by the Division of Christian Education of the National Council of Churches of Christ in the U.S.A. Used by permission. All rights reserved.

Cover design by Kathryn Brewer.

1	2	3	4	5	6	7	8	9

Library of Congress Cataloging-in-Publication Data

Upton, Julia.
    A time for embracing : reclaiming reconciliation / Julia Upton.
       p.   cm.
    Includes bibliographical references and index.
    ISBN 0-8146-2373-5 (alk. paper)
    1. Reconciliation—Religious aspects—Catholic Church.
  2. Catholic Church—Doctrines.   3. Confession.   I. Title.
    BX2265.2.U68   1999
    264'.02086—dc21   98-42627
                                              CIP

For the
Benedictine Community
of Glastonbury Abbey,
Hingham, Massachusetts,
whose hospitality of heart and hearth
has nurtured the writer within me

Contents

Acknowledgments

Despite whose name is on the cover, I doubt that any book is the product of one author alone. Similarly, I doubt whether anyone's attempt to acknowledge all the people who assisted in the process of producing a book is completely successful. In the context of the work at hand, however, I trust that those whom I might have inadvertently overlooked will forgive me.

Somewhere in elementary or secondary school I came to the conclusion that it was not good practice to ask questions. To ask questions in class, I observed, was to incur the wrath of teachers, who instantly concluded that the questioner had not been paying sufficient attention in class. Not wanting to appear "stupid," therefore, I rarely gave voice to the questions that rumbled within me.

My father, on the other hand, had different advice. "The stupid question is the one you didn't ask," he cautioned. However, I think I was already in college before I realized that my father's approach was the more appropriate one. He was responsible for my giving voice to all the questions that follow in the text, and had he lived to see this work finally completed, he would surely have reveled in the answers.

There have been many teachers along the way, but it was a treasured semester with Fr. Bernard Häring, C.Ss.R, at Fordham University that set me on this particular course. A man whom many would regard as the premier moral theologian of the twenty-first century, Father Häring helped me to develop an appreciation for the covenantal relations we each have with God. From him I learned that living the Christian life is less about obeying laws and getting it right than about developing and deepening one's relationship with God and others in the human community and always remaining open to the transformative power of grace. Father Häring did not just teach and write; he lived with an openness and love even when he was under attack. So far, he is the closest I have come to meeting Jesus.

And there have been students—thousands of them—whose questions over thirty years have prodded my thinking and whose stories have seeded my writing.

Most people are fortunate to have one community to rely on for support. I have been abundantly blessed, for there have been several communities that have supported me during the years I spent in researching and writing this book. The Institute of the Sisters of Mercy of the Americas, and the Brooklyn Regional Community in particular, have given me time and space to grow and to work. They remain a continual source of encouragement. The administration of St. John's University granted me a sabbatical year at the beginning of this project, which got me off to a running start, and the assistance of my colleagues Lisa Getman, Suzi Halpin, and Fran Fico has been invaluable in this project.

The monastic communities of Mount Saviour Monastery in Elmira, New York, and Glastonbury Abbey in Hingham, Massachusetts, have been praying with me and for me for many years and have welcomed me to the School for the Lord's service on many occasions. From them I slowly learned the discipline and pleasure of the writing life.

Surrounding me with good words and images is a wonderful community of artists and writers upon whom I have depended for inspiration and elevation. They include Joan Chittister, O.S.B., Virginia Farnan, R.S.M., Maura Flannery, Timothy Joyce, O.S.B., Jane Klimsch, O.S.B., Nathan Mitchell, Gertrud Mueller Nelson, Kathleen Norris, and Rembert Weakland, O.S.B. Finally, my family, by being the first to embrace me and by forgiving me again and again, helped to lay the groundwork for this present work.

Introduction

He had been held prisoner for seven years under the most despicable conditions, the details of which still make the strongest of us recoil in horror. Yet, when asked if he had any bitterness toward the people who held him captive for so long, Terry Anderson replied, "I don't have time for it. I don't have any need for it. It is required of me as a Christian to put that aside, to forgive them. I pray for them. I wish them no ill in their lives. My life is very, very busy—it is full of joy. The world is fresh and bright and beautiful."[1]

An enigma? I think not. As Saint Paul once said of the resurrection, however, in Mr. Anderson's witness we see a "stumbling block" for those who do not believe, but the power of God manifest in glory for those who do.

If there is anything enigmatic about Mr. Anderson's response, it is surely the grand silence that followed. No one seemed to follow up on it. The silence was so vacuous that one could almost hear the echoes of unvoiced thoughts: "He must be insane!" Instead, media focus quickly shifted to others who had been imprisoned, to get their reaction—months, even years, after their release. Forgiveness seems so un-American. It hardly squares with the cinema's idea of a hero these days. The American public would probably have been more comfortable with a hostage who had spent his seven years' imprisonment plotting the ultimate revenge.

Sin, confession, forgiveness, and reconciliation—the words themselves seem to be out of fashion, out of place today. They make us uncomfortable. Over the past several years I have been invited to speak to numerous catechumenal and parent groups about these concepts, preparing people for celebrating the rite of penance. In many instances, it seems to be the only subject catechists are reluctant to address themselves. Why? Has that always been so?

Thirty years ago I found myself in exactly the same spot that many catechists and presbyters find themselves in today. I was teaching in a parish elementary school, and since the school operated with a departmental structure rather than in self-contained classrooms, I was assigned to teach several sections of "Religion." In those days it was still the practice for children to "go to confession" before receiving their first communion. Confession was also part of the fourth-grade curriculum, but I felt woefully inadequate to teach children anything about it.

Fresh out of college, I was myself wrestling with the same questions my university students have today about the necessity of confessing one's sins to a priest, as if doing so somehow by-passed God. That was heavy-duty rationalization on my part, I admit, but I did not recognize it as such at the time. Aware of the tremendous hang-ups I had about guilt and scrupulosity, I was unwilling to hand those on to another generation. I told the priest who was assigned to visit the fourth grade that if he wanted the children to learn anything else about confession, he would have to teach them himself.

That admission humbled me, but it also hurled me in another direction, not away from the sacrament but into the sacrament. It sent me off to find answers to my questions, and that quest plunged me into the depths of mystery—the mystery of God's boundless mercy and forgiveness. Now, as one of the stewards of that mystery, I teach, speak, and write broadly about forgiveness and reconciliation, all the while continuing to plumb their depths.

What I have discovered in this quest is neither one-dimensional nor simplistic. Rather, there have been some curious conundrums at every turn. Let me cite a few.

Since the early 1970s many articles about the declining number of people going to confession have appeared in religious journals across the United States. On a recent trip to Ireland, therefore, I was astounded to see in a tourist brochure a listing of times not only for Mass at the local churches but also for confession. Two of the churches each "heard" confessions for three and a half hours on Saturdays, the other church for more than five hours. "But do people come?" I wondered. "In droves!" I was told. Why is it so different in the United States?

> Andrea, an inquirer, explained to Father Jim that she wanted to become a Catholic.
>
> "Why?" was his first question to her.
>
> "So that I can go to confession," she answered immediately.

In a day when fewer and fewer Catholics seem to be availing themselves of sacramental reconciliation, it seems ironic that this is the principal reason many people cite for seeking incorporation into the Roman Catholic community. What is this telling us?

"What are non-confessing Catholics doing with their guilt?" an article in *U.S. Catholic* asks.[2] The responses are both healthy and encouraging. Rather than ignoring their guilt, the people whose responses are recorded in this article dealt with their guilt head on. If they had harmed their relationship with another person and felt guilty, they went first to restore the relationship.

There are inevitable cuts and bruises in everyday life that affect our relationships with others, and the more intense our relationships, the more likely they are to be marred. Not every mark needs the medical intervention of sacramental reconciliation; some just need the soothing balm of love and the healing touch of the words, "I'm sorry for that; please forgive me." In fact, dashing off to confession to get Father's "forgiveness" will do nothing for the relationship that remains in need of our spiritual attention.

"Then, what would one bring to the Church for sacramental reconciliation?" you ask. Again, the medical analogy is helpful. Sometimes we have ruptures in our relationships that just will not heal, no matter what we do. No matter what we say or do to try to repair the damage, every time we look at the relationship it is bleeding. The counsel of the confessor and the prayer of the Church can help us in such a situation.

In the novel *A Thousand Acres*, author Jane Smiley narrates the story of what can happen when such wounds go untreated.

> Linda was just born when I had my first miscarriage, and for a while, six months maybe, the sight of those two

> babies, whom I had loved and cared for with real interest
> and satisfaction, affected me like a poison. All my tissues
> hurt when I saw them, and when I saw Rose with them,
> it was as if my capillaries were carrying acid into the fur-
> thest reaches of my system. I was so jealous, and so
> freshly jealous every time I saw them, that I could hardly
> speak, and I wasn't very nice to Rose, since some visceral
> part of me simply blamed her for having what I wanted,
> and for having it so easily. . . .[3]

What both of these situations demonstrates is the importance of bringing our sins and shortcomings into the light, and I am concerned that the sacrament of reconciliation—the sacrament through which the darkness of sin is illumined by the healing light of Christ's forgiveness—is an endangered species. Although they do not use the same terminology, that also seems to have been the conclusion of the Committee for Pastoral Research and Practices of the National Conference of Catholic Bishops, which published *Study of Penance* in 1990. The committee surveyed bishops, priests, and lay people regarding their personal understanding and use of the sacrament, as well as their thoughts on the practice of sacramental reconciliation in the United States. That data is presented in the text and analyzed in detail, and supports my conclusion that we have an "endangered" sacrament.

Let me be clear that my concern stems not from my being a fan of those spooky, dark confessionals some of us populated in the not-too-distant past, but rather from my belief that in sacraments we experience the real presence of God in our midst. In sacramental reconciliation the sinner experiences the tender, healing, welcoming embrace of God. That is what I regard as endangered.

One solution might be to mandate that everyone get back in line at the confessional, but I doubt that such an approach would be very effective. Better, I believe, would be a holistic approach to sacramental reconciliation. This would involve studying data from anthropology, psychology, and sociology, and integrating that with data from Scripture, history, and theology. After thirty years of study, it is obvious to me that this sacrament is endangered, not because people do not "go to confession," but because the sacrament is not understood or celebrated well.

If you track this analogy to other endangered species, you will have a better sense of the direction of this book. Conservationists teach us that preservation of any natural species involves more than noting the fact that the species is endangered. Beyond identifying the potential threat to its existence, we must first genuinely appreciate the species before we can adequately protect it. We cannot be expected to protect what we do not recognize to be of value. This is even truer when the protection of a species requires some alteration in people's behavior.

In the following pages, therefore, I propose to set out before the reader the sacrament of reconciliation so that it may be better appreciated. In Chapter 1 we will take a close look at the magnitude of the problem and identify some of its causes. From there, in Chapter 2, we will see the influence that contemporary American society has on our sacramental practice. Scripture will be the focus of Chapter 3, and in Chapter 4 we will examine the historical development of the sacrament. Chapter 5 will fill out the picture by providing a theological focus to the ritual celebration of the sacrament. The final chapter will then bring us to the brink of tomorrow with an invitation to action by suggesting ways in which we, as ambassadors of reconciliation, might alter the sacrament's fate.

Notes

1. David Aikman, "The World Is Fresh and Bright and Beautiful," interview with Terry Anderson, *Time* (May 18, 1992) 57–58.

2. "What Are Non-Confessing Catholics Doing with Their Guilt?" *U.S. Catholic* 50 (April 1985) 31–34.

3. Jane Smiley, *A Thousand Acres* (New York: Alfred A. Knopf, 1991) 8.

Chapter 1

Reconciliation at the Crossroads

"Whatever became of confession?" a sincere "practicing" Catholic asked me recently. His use of the past tense startled me at first, for his question seemed to imply that this sacrament of the Church had disappeared, or at least had been lost somewhere along the way.

Is his perception accurate? Has sacramental reconciliation disappeared from the horizon of Catholic practice? Has "confession" been extinguished from your practice of the faith? Has there been a marked change in the way in which we have become reconciled to God and the Church community over the course of time?

Surely when we compare sacramental practice today with what we knew a generation ago, it is obvious that a drastic change has taken place. In 1972 Francis Buckley, S.J., wrote, "During the last few years there has been a sharp drop in confession: about fifty percent in Europe and up to seventy-five percent in some parts of the United States."[1] With that as the state of affairs twenty-five years ago, what would similar statistics reveal today?

A survey of Catholic practice undertaken by the Committee for Pastoral Research and Practice of the National Conference of Catholic Bishops in 1988 reported that four percent of the laity surveyed celebrated the sacrament weekly; five percent monthly; 17 percent every two or three months; 55 percent once or twice a year; 19 percent never.[2] Because we do not have comparable statistics for 1958 or any other specific time period, we can draw conclusions based only on our perceptions of Catholic practice thirty years ago. Furthermore, since the survey did not question any of the respondents on their prior

1

experience with the sacrament and did not draw out their mystagogical reflections on becoming reconciled with God and community, we do not even have a complete picture of the state of the sacrament in 1988. This much seems obvious, however: people are simply not availing themselves of the sacrament of penance to the same degree they once did.

How well I remember Saturday after Saturday, anxiously waiting in those endless lines for a tense two minutes in the darkened confessional with a shadow-masked priest. Gone is the *angst,* gone are the confessional queues. Saturdays now find church buildings deserted, and we are left to ponder the questions that linger in the air:

> Has everyone stopped sinning?
>
> Aren't Catholics required to go to confession anymore?
>
> Where are all those people today?
>
> Is the *sensus fidelium* informing us that the sacrament of penance as we now know it is no longer fundamental to the life of Catholic Christians?
>
> Are we experiencing the dissolution or the transformation of this sacrament?

These questions are not mine alone, and there is evidence of considerable concern with regard to the issues they raise on all levels of Church leadership. The subject was discussed at the 1983 Synod of Bishops, and the following year Pope John Paul II issued the synod exhortation *Reconciliatio et Paenitentia.* Theologians and diocesan liturgical commissions continue to study the issue.[3] The problem is multifaceted and deeply rooted among us. More is required than issuing a directive that Catholics get back in the confession queue. We must begin with a serious attempt to understand the problem, if indeed it is a problem, for only then can the issues be analyzed properly.

An appropriate place to start, it would seem, is with the subject of sin in the present age, as unpopular or "un-American" as that might be in these closing days of the twentieth century. Furthermore, it is not enough to speak in abstract terms about sin, for sin, like love, does not exist in the abstract but only in the concrete reality of sinning. Without an adequate understanding of sin or awareness that one's relationship with God and the Church community has been disrupted, a person will never recognize a need for reconciliation.

The title of this chapter, "Reconciliation at the Crossroads," might at first glance appear to be very tranquil, bucolic even, and might even elicit echoes of Robert Frost's voice: "Two roads diverged in a leafy wood. . . ."[4] Let me remind you, however, that crossroads can also be dangerous intersections where cars can get mangled and people mutilated. Standing at this or any other crossroad requires that we be alert and look down the road in each direction. With that caveat in mind, we turn to the list of crossroad questions.

Sin at the Crossroads

Has everyone stopped sinning? Dr. Karl Menninger, who phrased the question a bit differently in his book *Whatever Became of Sin?*, examined the apparent disappearance of many forms of sin in our society. He concluded that "the present world miasma and depression are partly the result of our self-induced conviction that since sin has ceased to be, only the neurotics need to be treated and the criminals punished."[5] Acknowledging the reality of sin in our lives, he believed, was the only hopeful approach available to us. Those who are unable to face sin will be left to read the newspapers, look at television, do their own thing, and keep their "eye on the road leading to the main chance."[6]

Here we have a psychiatrist, not a "theologian" per se, observing and responding to a cultural phenomenon by pointing out for us the importance of facing the different levels of sin that insidiously eat away at the roots of our humanity—personal sin, communal sin, social sin or "collective irresponsibility," and sins against humanity.

"Sin is more than the sum of what sinners do," writes theologian Cornelius Plantinga as he vividly describes the insidiousness of sin. "Sin acquires the powerful and elusive form of a spirit—the spirit of an age or a company or a nation or a political movement. Sin burrows into the bowels of institutions and traditions, making a home there and taking them over."[7]

When I was a child growing up in the 1950s, I thought I knew exactly what sin was and could rattle off definitions with ease. As I emerged from adolescence into adulthood, however, I became less sure of my memorized definitions and of myself.

Was I alone in my confusion? Actually, the *Study Document* of the Committee for Pastoral Research and Practices reflects similar confusion among Catholics. Laity surveyed were asked to select from a list of statements the three that best described their personal view of sin. The statements were:

1. Disobeying God's law or that of the Church

2. Injuring myself or another

3. Saying "no" to God

4. Not living up to my potential (laziness)

5. Indifference to the suffering of others (apathy)

6. Wounding the Church, the Body of Christ

7. Striving to go beyond my potential despite cost to self and others (pride and ambition)

8. Loss of God's grace

9. Refusal to love

10. Selfishness

According to the *Study Document*, the three most frequently chosen statements were numbers 1, 3, and 8. From this selection, the report concludes, it would seem that people do not understand or have a vocabulary to express the ecclesial or social dimensions of sin.

Surely this cannot be surprising. Before one can develop any vocabulary, one needs to be exposed to words, and by appearing to speak of "sin" almost exclusively as personal failure to obey laws and limiting it to the sphere of sexuality, the Church fails to encourage appropriate vocabulary development and conscience formation. The Church's social teaching, referred to by some theologians as its best kept secret,[8] would certainly help to broaden the average Catholic's vocabulary of sin, but this aspect of sin rarely makes either the evening news or the Sunday homily.

Recall the lawyer who tried to disconcert Jesus one day by inquiring about the "bottom line" for eternal life. Jesus turned the question right around to him.

"What is written in the law? What do you read there?"

The lawyer replied, "You shall love the Lord your God with all your heart, and with all your soul, and with all your strength, and with all your mind; and your neighbor as yourself."

Jesus responded, "You have given the right answer; do this, and you will live" (Luke 10:27-28).[9]

Notice that *law* is not the issue here; *relationships* are. Sin, therefore, is not about violating laws as much as it is about violating relationships—relationships with ourselves, God, and others. These violations, obviously, can vary in severity, but they are what constitute the "ecclesial dimension" of sin.

Do you remember the capital or deadly sins, which have found their way from catechisms into literature, movies, and theater? I always think of them as the most "deadly" because of the way in which we snarled them out: pride, covetousness, lust, anger, gluttony, envy, and sloth.[10] Putting them back into the context in which we learned them, however, we see that they were called "capital," not because they in themselves are the greatest sins, but rather because they are the chief reasons why people commit sin.[11] In other words, they are the source of sins, not sins in themselves, although the confusion persisted because they were still called "sins."

When you look at the list again, you notice that the seven deadly sins are not primarily actions but feelings or desires. Pop psychologists have made millions of dollars teaching us that feelings are healthy emotional responses to given stimuli.[12]

If someone cuts us off on the road, it is appropriate to experience a flash of anger. What we do with our anger, however, is quite a different matter, and when we allow that emotional response to affect our relationships—with ourselves, God, or others—we move into the arena of sin.

In the *Baltimore Catechism* each of those capital sins was "balanced off" with a virtue to which it was opposed.[13] The list would look something like this:

Capital Sin		Virtue
Pride	balanced by	Humility
Covetousness		Justice
Lust		Chastity
Anger		Meekness
Gluttony		Temperance
Envy		Charity
Sloth		Charity

The danger is that this schema creates the illusion that one cultivates these virtues if one "just says no" to the capital sins. That, of course, is denial, not virtue, and it amounts to a sin against ourselves because it denies our own reality.

Take the situation of a colleague getting a big promotion and a huge salary increase. Feeling envious would hardly be a surprising response. Rather than deny the feeling or feign happiness at another's good fortune, however, it would be better to look within our conscience for the real source of that envy. Perhaps it is dissatisfaction with our job, or debts we have assumed, or frustration at not advancing ourselves, for example, that is actually at the root of our envy and simply triggered by another's good fortune. Virtue will only develop when we address the root causes of the deadly sins, and denial, when it goes unchecked, just might be the most deadly sin of all.

Actually, the *Baltimore Catechism* had some sound advice to give us. It stated:

> We can keep from committing sin by praying and receiving the sacraments; by remembering that God is always with us; by recalling that our bodies are temples of the Holy Ghost; by keeping occupied with work or play; by promptly resisting the sources of sin within us; by avoiding the near occasions of sin.[14]

It is important, however, for us to look at this statement in context, because although much of it is good advice, it poses some difficulties as well.

The first difficulty here is the placement of this "advice" in the *Baltimore Catechism*. It follows the discussion of actual sin and the delineation of mortal and venial sins, and answers the question, "How can we keep from committing sin?" The discussion of capital sins comes later. Because this advice was placed before the discussion of capital sins, students unconsciously concluded that the only hope they had of overcoming anger, lust, envy, etc., was by denying them.

We now know that nothing could be farther from the truth. People who are emotionally healthy will continue to have all those feelings. No matter how many years one has been happily married, when a physically attractive person crosses one's path, one has a feeling response. That does not necessarily indicate that there is a problem with the marriage; rather, it probably means that there is something right with the married person. (This has been a great comfort to my undergraduate students, who are just beginning to look objectively at interpersonal relationships.) We know when we cross the line. Having lustful feelings does not violate fidelity or chastity; voyeurism does.

Look at the "advice" list again. Notice that praying and receiving the sacraments come first. To it I would link the next item: remembering that God is always with us. Saint Paul, one of the great saints and sinners of all time, reminds us in his Letter to the Romans that Christ died for us while we were still sinners and that God's grace is far greater than any of our sins.[15]

Recognizing our human frailty should draw us into a deeper relationship with God. Too often we run away and hide instead. John Bradshaw has concluded from his study of human behavior that we run away because we have been "shamed" and cannot own responsibility for our actions. He distinguishes between toxic shame and healthy shame. Toxic shame alienates us from ourselves, and consequently from God, in whose image we have been created. Healthy shame, by contrast, is actually a source of spirituality, continually reminding us of our need for God.[16]

"Recalling that our bodies are temples of the Holy Ghost" really means remembering the God in whose image we were "fearfully and wonderfully made," in the words of Psalm 139. Who are we to deny the beauty of God's creation?

Unfortunately, many of us have taken the advice of "keeping ourselves occupied with work or play" to the extreme and now find ourselves addicted to any number of substances or processes. Obviously, this is not healthy either but is rather another cloak of denial.

Perhaps now we have a better answer to the original question, "Has everyone stopped sinning?" Hardly! Any cursory reading of the daily newspaper or weekly news magazine will quickly demonstrate that idolatry is one sin that overwhelms us personally, communally, and socially. We appear to worship the products of our own hands and have alienated ourselves from one another in competition and in the struggle for possession and profit. Alienated from our own humanness, we have become transformed into the idols we trust, and the compulsion to consume controls us.[17]

No, sin has not disappeared. The names will be different: addiction in all shapes and sizes, consumerism, militarism, sexism . . . the list will go on and on. Sin is still with us, and so too is God, who has promised us mercy.

Confession at the Crossroads

Our second question was, "Aren't Catholics required to go to confession anymore?" In the mid to late 1960s, when Saturday confession lines began to disappear, it was not because people had stopped sinning or had decided to become scofflaws. No one gave Catholics permission to stop going to confession—they just did. Society was changing, images of God were changing, and these radically affected previously unquestioned patterns of confessing sin.

Technology, by way of sophisticated satellite communications, moved the world right into our homes overnight. Rather than having Movietone News summarize world events for us, we had the Vietnam War fought in our living rooms. We walked on the moon with Neil Armstrong, sat stunned as Challenger exploded before our eyes, and saw the bombs shower on Baghdad during the sanitized Gulf War. No longer are we shielded, even for an hour, from either the triumph or the suffering of the human community.[18] In the face of all this, it is not surprising that the Saturday ritual of confessing the same sins week after week would begin to seem meaningless—an immature holdover from a previous era. For some, this led to latent conscience maturation; for others, to continued confusion about what actually constitutes sin.[19]

This phenomenon was accompanied by our changing concept of God. Perhaps it was high technology that began in the 1960s to transform God from a pseudo-benevolent despot to a loving parent, but I see it more directly as a result of our beginning to celebrate Eucharist in our native tongue. Once we began to ponder our sinfulness in the penitential rite, to pray the Lord's Prayer in common, and to exchange the kiss of peace, we became more aware of other meaningful ways in which we are reconciled with God and with one another.

The *Baltimore Catechism* taught that the sacrament of penance was necessary only for the forgiveness of mortal sins. Venial sins, we learned, could be forgiven in other ways, in particular through devout reception of Eucharist. Yet, week after week we lined up to confess the same list of venial sins, just to be sure that they were forgiven or perhaps to get extra grace. Today, before approaching the altar to receive Eucharist, the assembly, as with one voice, faithfully and urgently prays, "Lord, I am not worthy to receive you, but only say the word and I shall be healed." A generation ago the very same phrase was mumbled in Latin, "Domine, non sum dignus ut intres sub tectum meum, sed tantum dic verbo et sanabitur anima mea." The effect is not the same. With the vernacular came transformation, and as a result today we believe and experience God's loving mercy more confidently.

In the early 1960s the tone of articles about confession appearing in religious magazines in the United States shifted. The assurance that devotional confessions were a practice to be encouraged began to wane as questions about the ecclesial dimensions of this practice grew. The image of Church as the people of God, so central to the documents of Vatican Council II, had begun to emerge in Europe in the decades leading to the Council, and American theologians who had studied abroad began to raise serious questions about sacramental practice on this side of the Atlantic.

Reports began to spread in the United States about what was happening in other countries with regard to the sacrament of penance. The April 5, 1962, issue of the *Catholic Messenger,* for example, carried an article reporting on public celebrations of the sacrament of penance taking place in France and the Netherlands. Writing in *Paroisse et Liturgie* (May 1962), Dom Thierry Maertens of the Abbey of Saint-André in Bruges, Belgium, described in great detail a communal service used in the Archdiocese of Malines there.[20]

During Advent in 1976, Bishop Carroll T. Dozier of Memphis, Tennessee, made headlines in the United States when he presided over reconciliation services at which thirteen thousand Catholics, over one-quarter of the Memphis diocese, experienced the embrace of forgiveness in sacramental reconciliation. The mood was exciting, electrifying even. As shepherd of Memphis's Catholics, Bishop Dozier was most concerned about inactive Catholics, particularly those who for personal or psychological reasons were unable to take the first step in returning to the Church. He wanted the rite of penance to be a bridge, an "extended hand."[21]

I remember clearly the first communal penance service I ever attended. It was during Lent of 1972, when I was not a very active Catholic myself. I read about the upcoming service in our parish bulletin. Intrigued by the concept and drawn by guilt, I arrived at the parish church that Saturday afternoon. The church was filled with people, and because there was no "official" form of a communal rite of penance at that time, the ritual took the shape of a liturgy of the word focused on sin and repentance, a communal examination of conscience, individual confessions, concluding with common absolution. It was very much like the service described in Belgium ten years earlier and an accurate response to the reform mandated by Vatican Council II. "The rite and formulas of Penance are to be revised so that they more clearly express both the nature and effect of the sacrament."[22] These celebrations gave clear expression to the Church's witness that God welcomes the repentant sinner, a cause for rejoicing, not shame.

My dad had a dictum, "Praise in public, criticize in private." It is regrettable that such earthy wisdom was not followed by Church officials in their outright condemnation of Bishop Dozier's celebrations or in the thousands of other reverent and faith-filled celebrations of the third form of the rite of penance.[23]

The Memphis program, in preparation for several months, began with the Advent celebrations and continued through the Easter season. Confessors were named and regional sites specified for all those interested in private consultation with a confessor following general absolution. Careful to nuance this recommendation, Bishop Dozier believed that "the grace of the sacrament will take care of them from then on. . . . I am counting on Jesus being there and I'm counting on him doing his job. I'm counting on that spark in human nature that really wants to know and love God."[24] He certainly followed the norms of the Spirit outlined in the Acts of the Apostles. In addition to an extensive education, a day of prayer and Eucharistic adoration were held in every parish. Several days before the first celebration, the entire diocese observed a day of prayer and fasting, and the bishop prepared himself by an eight-day retreat.[25]

Two decades later, I can see no better model for a diocese to adopt. It gives vivid ritual expression to the circumstances of sin, penance, and reconciliation as described in the *Catechesim of the Catholic Church*. There we read that "sin is before all else an offense against God, a rupture of communion with him. At the same time it damages communion with the Church. For this reason conversion entails both God's forgiveness and reconciliation with the Church. . . ."[26]

In my work as a university professor, trying to educate and prepare young men and women for their role in the Church of tomorrow, I have given much attention to the pastoral situation of sacramental reconciliation today. That has led me to many parish settings where I have presented workshops on the sacrament of reconciliation, both for general audiences and for the parents of children preparing for first Eucharist. In working with adults preparing for entrance into full communion with the Roman Catholic Church, I have also had the privilege of participating in the process of catechesis. Each of these three groups has a different agenda, one might say, but the core issues remain the same: fear, confusion, and discomfort.

Why do we think it should be different? Using Annie Dillard's words: "Week after week we witness the same miracle: that God, for reasons unfathomable, refrains from blowing our dancing bear act to smithereens. Week after week Christ washes the disciples' dirty feet, handles their very toes, and repeats, It is all right—believe it or not—to be people. Who can believe it?"[27]

In *Megatrends,* John Naisbitt introduced his readers to the "high tech/high touch" formula, which posits that the more advanced our technology becomes, the greater is our need for a counterbalancing human response.[28] It is immediately obvious to people with a good pastoral sense that in the sacrament of penance we have the possibility of a high-touch sacrament at a deeply spiritual level. Following that principle, and given the technological intensity that pervades our world, it would seem that our need for the sacrament of penance today is even greater than it was a generation ago.

Where Have All the People Gone?

When we return to the data in the bishops' survey of pastoral practice, we see that the answers differ according to who is asked the question. The *Study Document* notes that one of the strongest points of divergence centers on reasons given for the decline in reception of the sacrament of penance. The bishops most often cite "a less pervasive sense of sin" as the reason for the decline. The priests regard "general confusion over what is right or wrong" as the principal reason. The people, however, respond that decline is the result of "reconciliation experienced by other means." Furthermore, the laity list in seventh place the reasons given first preference by both bishops and priests. The *Study Document* does not list the selections given second, third, or fourth ranking by the laity. It is important that we pay attention to that data.

In this age of technology we see that therapy, spiritual direction, and specialized support groups now fill a need that was once met by periodic confession.[29] This trend, which began in the early 1970s, when pop psychology books began to head the best-seller lists with increasing regularity, continues strongly today. Rather than viewing this development negatively, however, we ought to be able to recognize in it the beginnings of collective maturation and healthy conscience-formation. Such a trend will not threaten the sacrament of reconciliation but has the possibility of helping to restore it to full vigor.[30]

Sensus Fidelium

The fourth question is even thornier: Is the *sensus fidelium* informing us that the sacrament of penance as we now know it is no longer fundamental to the life of Catholic Christians? One way of answering that question is to return to the data presented by the Bishops' Committee for Pastoral Research and Practice. When asked to identify from a list of eighteen items all the ways in which they "have experienced God's reconciliation, forgiveness, and healing grace apart from the celebration of the sacrament of penance,"[31] the most common responses given were:

Means of Experiencing Reconciliation (apart from the Sacrament of Penance)
84% Eucharist
78% Personal prayer
64% Acts of contrition
52% Conversation with a friend
45.8% Works of mercy
45.2% Reading the Scriptures[32]

Vatican Council II's Dogmatic Constitution on the Church *(Lumen gentium)* refers to the Church as a sacrament of reconciliation, an instrument for achieving unity with God and the unity of the human family.[33] Confession of sins is but one moment in the process of sacramental reconciliation, which forms but a small part of the Church's ministry of reconciliation:

> The people of God accomplish and perfect this continual repentance in many different ways. They share in the sufferings of Christ by enduring their own difficulties, carry

out works of mercy and charity, and adopt ever more
fully the outlook of the Gospel message. Thus the people of
God become in the world a sign of conversion to God.[34]

The *sensus fidelium* seems to be confirming what the bishops at
Vatican Council II stated clearly thirty years ago. Our fixation
on the confession of sins in the recent past actually blinded us
to the larger process of reconciliation.

It is surprising when we study the history of the sacrament
of penance, which we will examine in more detail in Chapter
Four, to note its rather late development. Canonical or public
penance didn't emerge in the Church's practice until the third
century. Prior to that time, the Church did not allow for the
reconciliation of sinners after baptism. Private individual confession as we know it didn't gain official Church approval
until the Fourth Lateran Council in 1215.

When we look to the ministry of Jesus and compare it with
the early Church's apparent refusal to readmit sinners, it seems
as though the apostles' successors were violating an essential
principle of Jesus' life and work. We must remember, however,
that becoming a Christian in the early centuries was a much
more involved process and only followed upon three or four
years of intensive preparation. Although the rite of penance
might not have existed per se, the Church certainly did allow
for reconciliation of sinners. The sacrament of reconciliation in
those days, however, was baptism.

There was also a greater appreciation in the early days of
Christianity for the Eucharist as a sacrament of reconciliation.
While canonical penance, from the third century on, was a
method for reconciling those guilty of grave sin, the general
Christian population was reconciled to God and to the community during the Eucharistic meal. The penitential rite was
an element that appeared in Eucharistic celebrations as early
as the second century.[35]

Reaffirming and clearly teaching that both baptism and Eucharist are also sacraments of reconciliation will not rob the
rite of penance of its place in the life of the Church. Rather, it
will restore to sacramental reconciliation its proper place in
the sacramental continuum.

The foregoing data actually provide only a partial answer to the fourth question. Hidden within the response "conversation with a friend," I suspect, is a much broader indicator of how people are actually experiencing reconciliation with God, self, neighbor, and Church.

The perceived meaninglessness of our old patterns of confession has been addressed in the revised ritual, but full implementation still awaits solid catechesis on reconciliation and its place in our lives today.[36] The burgeoning phenomenon of support groups tells another part of the story. In the next chapter we will take a closer look at that dimension of reconciliation.

Dissolution or Transformation?

Finally, we turn to the last question: Are we experiencing the dissolution or the transformation of this sacrament? That is surely the key question of the moment, but asking the question is a long way from accumulating the data needed to answer it. That, in fact, will be our enterprise in succeeding chapters, as we examine the culture, Scripture, history, and sacramental rituals. Only then will it be appropriate to return to this most serious question.

Notes

1. Francis J. Buckley, S.J., *"I Confess": The Sacrament of Penance Today* (Notre Dame: Ave Maria, 1972) 21.

2. Committee for Pastoral Research and Practices, National Conference of Catholic Bishops, *Reflections on the Sacrament of Penance in Catholic Life Today: A Study Document* (Washington, D.C.: National Conference of Catholic Bishops, 1990) 7. [Hereafter referred to as *Study Document.*]

3. For a good cross section, see the essays in *Reconciliation: The Continuing Agenda,* ed. Robert J. Kennedy (Collegeville: The Liturgical Press, 1987); *Reconciling Embrace: Foundations for the Future of Sacramental Reconciliation,* ed. Robert J. Kennedy (Chicago: Liturgy Training Publications, 1998).

4. Robert Frost, "The Road Not Taken," *The Poetry of Robert Frost,* ed. Edward Connery Lathem (New York: Holt, Rinehart and Winston, 1969) 105.

5. Karl Menninger, M.D., *Whatever Became of Sin?* (New York: Hawthorn Books, 1973) 188.

6. Ibid.

7. Cornelius Plantinga, Jr., *Not the Way It's Supposed to Be: A Breviary of Sin* (Grand Rapids, Mich.: Eerdmans, 1995) 75.

8. See Peter J. Henriot, Edward P. De Berri, and Michael J. Shultheis, *Catholic Social Teaching: Our Best Kept Secret* (Maryknoll, N.Y.: Orbis Books, 1990).

9. All Scripture references are to the New Revised Standard Version of the Holy Bible (New York: Oxford University Press, 1989).

10. Rev. Francis J. Connell, C.S.S.R., *Baltimore Catechism* No. 3 (New York: Benziger, 1949, 1952) no. 74. The *Catechism of the Catholic Church* [CCC] (Washington, D.C.: United States Catholic Conference, 1994) is now the authoritative reference. Although it serves more as a compendium of Church teachings than a précis as the *Baltimore Catechism* was, cross-references to the CCC will be given where applicable [CCC, no. 1886].

11. *Baltimore Catechism,* no. 75 [CCC, no. 1886].

12. For an important discussion on the effects of this confusion, see Richard Gula, *To Walk Together Again: The Sacrament of Reconciliation* (New York: Paulist Press, 1984) as well as the original essay on which it is based: John W. Glaser, "Conscience and Super-ego: A Key Distinction," *Theological Studies* 32 (1971) 30–47.

13. *Baltimore Catechism,* nos. 74a-g.

14. Ibid., no. 73.

15. Chapter 5 of the Letter to the Romans is a good source of meditation.

16. John Bradshaw, *Healing the Shame That Binds You* (Deerfield Beach, Fla.: Health Communications, 1988).

17. John Francis Kavanaugh, *Following Christ in a Consumer Society: The Spirituality of Cultural Resistance* (Maryknoll, N.Y.: Orbis, 1981) 11.

18. See John Naisbitt, *Megatrends: Ten New Directions Transforming Our Lives* (New York: Warner Books, 1984) 14–19; he refers to this as the demise of the "information float."

19. See Gula, *To Walk Together Again,* 89–136.

20. Cited in Frank B. Norris, S.S., "Reform of the Rite of Penance: Public Celebration and Confessions of Devotion," *Worship* 37 (January 1963) 107.

21. For a complete account of the diocesan program, see Albert Kirk, "Reconciliation in Memphis: A Diocese Prepared," *America* 136 (February 19, 1977) 146–148.

22. Constitution on the Sacred Liturgy *(Sacrosanctum Concilium),* no. 72, in Austin Flannery, O.P., ed., *Vatican Council II: The Basic Sixteen Documents*, rev. trans. (Northport, N.Y.: Costello Publishing Co., 1966). All quotations from the documents of Vatican II are taken from this edition.

23. See "General Absolution: Were the Norms Followed in Memphis?" *Origins* 7 (May 26, 1977) 1, 3–4.

24. Mark Winiarski, "Reconciliation in Memphis," *National Catholic Reporter* 13 (December 17, 1976) 3.

25. Kirk, "Reconciliation in Memphis," 148.

26. CCC, no. 1440.

27. Annie Dillard, *Teaching a Stone to Talk* (New York: Harper & Row, 1982) 20.

28. Naisbitt, *Megatrends,* 35–52.

29. See Kenneth Leech, *Soul Friend* (San Francisco: Harper & Row, 1980) 194–225.

30. Karl Rahner, "Problems Concerning Confession," *Theological Investigations* 3 (Baltimore: Helicon Press, 1968) 205.

31. Committee for Pastoral Research and Practices, National Conference of Catholic Bishops, *Pastoral Renewal and Penance: Questionnaire for the Penitent,* items 41–58.

32. *Study Document,* 8.

33. Dogmatic Constitution on the Church *(Lumen gentium)* no. 11.

34. *Rite of Penance,* no. 4 [hereafter cited as RP].

35. See *Didache,* chap. 14.

36. See M. Francis Mannion, "Penance and Reconciliation: A Systemic Analysis," *Worship* 60 (1986) 98–119.

Chapter 2

Reconciliation in American Society Today

> American Catholics are in the process of becoming more
> characteristically American than characteristically Catho-
> lic. Individualism compromises the contemporary prac-
> tice of ritual prayer . . . and further threatens to dissolve
> distinctly Catholic identity.[1]

Because of my growing concern and interest in the theology
of reconciliation, this conclusion of Mark Searle's prompted me
to test his hypothesis in a variety of ways among my university
students over the course of the last ten years. Two exercises
were particularly instructive.

The Human Family?

"Do you see yourself as *part of* the human family or *apart
from* the human family?" Early in the semester I generally address that question to the students enrolled in the Spirituality
course. An interesting discussion follows, sometimes encouraging, occasionally frightening, but always enlightening. While
many of the students do have a sense that there is a common
humanity—the human family—their number seems always
surprisingly small to me, given the technology that enables us
to encounter the world today in so many varied ways.

"Is there anything that everyone in the human family ought
to be guaranteed?" I then ask.

Inevitably someone in the class will respond with the proverbial American answer, "Life, liberty and the pursuit of happiness."

"Does that include food?" I further inquire.
Too often they aren't sure, and I wonder why.

Life Beyond Mr. Rogers' Neighborhood

"The one thing I fear most is _____."
When asked to complete that statement, students ten years ago usually wrote "death." Now their response is more likely to be "failure."

In an attempt to track down this growing fear of failure in young people, one semester I engaged in a somewhat haphazard survey of available student populations. Groups of twenty-five first graders, third graders, seventh graders, tenth graders, and college students were asked to answer the following questions:

Who is the most successful person you know?

Are you a success?

If so, why?

If you aren't a success now, do you think you ever will be one?

What is your favorite TV program?

"Mommy" was the most successful person on almost every first grader's horizon, with two "Daddies" making the list and one "Grandpa."

All of the first graders saw themselves as successful, and for a variety of wonderful reasons: "because I can read"; "because I try"; "because I'm kind"; "because I do my work."

As the children aged, learned more, and progressed in school, however, they progressively felt less successful and less sure that they would ever be successful. Simultaneously their concept of success came to be more dependent on financial wealth. Olympic athletes did not head their lists nor was a single one ever cited, but sports figures who had signed multimillion dollar, long-term contracts did, along with a representative smattering of celebrities from the music industry and even a number of gangsters. The only exceptions to that trend, in fact, were tenth graders raised in single-parent households headed by women, who once again considered their mothers to be successful for managing family and job without other support.

What happens to those bright inquiring minds that once asked such amazing questions as "Where do butterflies go in the rain?" As Walter Truett Anderson astutely observes in his book, *Reality Isn't What It Used to Be,* there is a cast of cultural critics ready to diagnose the cause for this crisis in our culture.[2] While one critic diagnoses us as suffering from narcissism, another declares us to be culturally illiterate. It has been determined by one critic that the American mind has been closed, just as yet another team of researchers concluded that the habits of our hearts have led us into the dark valley of individualism and despair. Each, as you might expect, has the appropriate antidote, which is cheered or jeered accordingly.

With the critics' voluminous data, stellar credentials, and convincing arguments, it might seem arrogant for me to be critiquing their work. As a theologian, however, I see something even more insidious eating away at our souls. The sociologists, I conclude, are still treating symptoms. I suggest that we need more aggressive intervention and therapy because the disease has run rampant in the culture too long.

What Has Happened to Us?

It would probably take several more studies of the stature of Dr. Menninger's[3] to uncover all of the reasons for our "self-induced conviction" that sin is irrelevant to our lives, but for the sake of the discussion at hand, let me focus on two reasons that appear to be immediately obvious to me.

The first reason I would label as past fixations, and into this category I would place the unformed, deformed, and ill-informed consciences of all those people whose moral development was fixated on the sixth and ninth commandments, and consequently arrested in pre-adolescence. This is precisely the issue we discussed in the last chapter.

The second reason I would label as disownership of responsibility, and into this category I would place what often seems to be our American propensity for passing the buck. From childhood on, people in general seem to have great difficulty in accepting responsibility for their actions, living instead by what they smugly refer to as the eleventh commandment— "Don't get caught!"

We could struggle forever to come up with an adequate definition of sin, but sin exists despite our ability or inability to define it. The face of sin changes over the course of time, however, and if we don't root it out of our personal, communal, and societal lives, it will destroy us. Saint Augustine described sin as "a turning away from the universal whole to the individual part."[4] John Kavanaugh, in his classic work, *Following Christ in a Consumer Society*, describes it as turning away from the personal form and into the commodity form[5]—different words for different eras, but the reality and its effects are the same.

In the two decades since Dr. Menninger asked that now proverbial question, it seems to me that rather than rooting out the causes of sin, we have been doing the converse—reading our newspapers, watching TV, and doing our own thing. This, I believe, is the contemporary equivalent of fiddling while Rome burns. Before we are burned alive and our humanity utterly destroyed, we need to take an honest look at ourselves, our community, and the larger society to see how sin has afflicted us.

The Paradigm Shifts

The term "paradigm shift" has found its way into many conversations today. The concept was developed by Thomas Kuhn a generation ago to explain how scientific progress takes place. Rather than moving ahead in a mechanical, linear fashion, the scientific community more characteristically lurches ahead in response to the creative bursts he called paradigm shifts.[6] The phenomenon observed by Kuhn in his segment of the scientific community as a leap into a new way of thinking is now recognized by social scientists as well. When sociologists, therefore, speak of a paradigm shift, they are referring to a cultural leap into a new way of living. In the Church, similarly, we can surely see that Vatican Council II effected just such a paradigm shift.

Wendell Berry, without using the term paradigm shift, saw exactly this phenomenon occurring in the United States. He termed it the cultural unsettling of America and expressed it in agricultural terms. Contrasting two approaches to life—exploitation and nurture—he conceived a strip miner to be a model exploiter and a farmer as a model nurturer.[7] He further observed that the first casualties of the exploitative revolution are character and community, for the first principle of the exploitative mind is to divide and conquer. I completely concur with his observation that "surely there has never been a people more ominously and painfully divided than we are—both against each other and within ourselves."[8] Divisiveness and a divided self, as we concluded in the first chapter, are sure signs of the presence of sin and our need for reconciliation.

Following Berry's trajectory, I see the cultural paradigm in slightly different terms. We appear to have abandoned the agricultural model and perpetuated the worst aspects of the industrial model. We must be caught in a time warp, hurled backward into the most dire conditions of the Industrial Revolution. I observe:

—a growing gulf between the rich and the poor

—homelessness increasing everywhere

—the disappearance of jobs

—significant unemployment

—longer working hours for less money

—a lengthening work week

—both spouses working

—children caring for themselves

—increasingly unaffordable healthcare

—the return of previously conquered diseases associated with poverty—tuberculosis, for example

—the disappearance of leisure time

Yes, it all has a Dickensian flavor to it.

Is this cycle inevitable or can we break out of it? To answer that question, we first need to look behind those dire condi-

tions, the symptoms of this social disease, to see what is caus-
ing them.

Although there are innumerable causes, let us begin by fo-
cusing our discussion on three that are ultimately attacks on
faith, hope, and charity: public opinion, technology, and greed.

Triumph of the Public

In the last three decades the laws of God and the laws of history have gradually been replaced by the laws of public opinion. Apparently the collective beliefs of people have now
become the repository of social reality.[9] Let us look at a few
examples of this shift.

Using one of those unwritten and now-disposed of laws of
history, the United States press corps during World War II decided not to film President Franklin Delano Roosevelt in his
wheelchair in case it might compromise his ability to command respect and to function as Commander in Chief of the
Armed Forces. Today we seem to have gone to the opposite
extreme, intentionally holding leaders up to public ridicule for
the sake of a few good laughs. Within ten days of his inaugu-
ration, the press was already evaluating Bill Clinton's first-
term presidency. Compromising the President's ability to
command respect no longer seems to be our concern.

We no longer look to the Church or the synagogue for inter-
pretations of human activity. Instead, information and explanations of "how things are" are fragmented and diversified,
spread throughout cultural agencies. Today, science, government, technology, business, labor, education, and the arts are
all autonomous, free from the dictates of religion.[10]

The converse also seems to be true: the media mediates the
Church to us as well, making some religious figures appear as
buffoons and others as idols. What is operative here is not a
law of God or a law of history or even what we used to know
as the simple law of good taste, but what we could call the
entertainment factor. We read excerpts of papal pronounce-
ments in the daily newspapers, but excerpts with public rather
than theological appeal. The media reports what sells, and
these days sex sells better than anything else.

The so-called sexual revolution of the 1960s reflected the shift as well. Although numerous studies now show that no dramatic revolution in sexuality took place in the 1960s,[11] it is true that there is an increasing permissiveness in both attitude and behavior today. Behavior that would have been labeled promiscuous a generation ago is now not only merely tolerated but actually encouraged by the laws of public opinion. College students often think it is required for a couple to live together before marrying, and it is quite common for men and women making arrangements for their wedding with the parish priest to give him the same address. The furor once occasioned by the miniskirt has virtually given way to an "anything goes" attitude. Public nudity seems to be the one holdout, but a student at the University of California-Berkeley recently tested even that as an infringement on his right to free speech. Just these few examples evidence a shift in the locus of authority from God to self.

The clearest case, however, surrounds the issue of abortion. If you listen carefully to the rhetoric, you will hear that it usually centers on concerns for privacy, not on the common good. The developing fetus is regularly spoken of as part of the woman's body—hers to dispose of at will. What happened to all of those lofty concepts of the children being our hope for the future? Is that hope now disposable? This surely seems to be a function of the strip-mining model rather than the nurturing model.

How did this come to be? It is important for us to address that question before we can have any hope of turning away from sin and putting our trust once again in the gospel.

Triumph of the Therapeutic

The topics of addiction and recovery are in vogue these days. A short excursion to your local bookstore will give you a good idea of what has been developing in psychological circles with the burgeoning number of books on addiction issues. The bandwagon is rolling, everyone seems to be climbing aboard, and it is getting very crowded. Notable among these are the books by Anne Wilson Schaef,[12] which continue to develop themes she originally presented in *Women's Reality*.[13] There was also the immense popularity of John Bradshaw's series, "On the Family," which was originally broadcast on PBS stations across the United States in 1987 and continues to be replayed to great acclaim. The series resulted in the subsequent publication of several books developing the same theme of healing the shame that binds us.[14]

While many people are climbing aboard that bandwagon, buying up books and probably to a lesser extent looking into their personal lives and into society as an addict, there are many who find the term "addictive society" to be too harsh. Still others find it to be a more euphemistic companion to the term "dysfunctional family." If we are uncomfortable with this conversation applied to our personal lives, the discomfort reaches the extreme when we begin to examine the Church in the same light. There was outrage when Matthew Fox published an essay in the *National Catholic Reporter* that examined the Church as a dysfunctional family,[15] and there was a similar reaction to Michael Crosby's work.[16]

I am approaching these concepts neither as a psychologist nor a sociologist, but rather as a theologian. I am reading the data and studying that data as it relates to the Church's understanding of sacramental theology, and in particular to the practice of sacramental reconciliation and the apparent decline of that practice.

I am also reading the data as a member of this so-called "addicted society," for I have come to see how our addiction binds us, blinds us, and keeps us from experiencing healthy relationships with one another and with God, who loves us unconditionally. Along with Anne Wilson Schaef, I see that while our planet is being destroyed, we respond with malaise, buying up anti-depressants instead of acting responsibly. Apathy and depression seem to have become synonymous with "adjustment."

As gospel people, we are in desperate need of being reconciled personally and sacramentally, although we might question whether or not those two terms can even be separated. Ironically, we need this reconciliation at the very time when ecclesial communities seem to be distancing themselves more and more from sacramental reconciliation.

In this chapter, we will first take a brief look at the concept of addiction, the characteristics of addictive behavior, and the dynamics of the addicted society, and then examine how they relate to our subject—the shape that sin, confession, and reconciliation take in such a society. Finally, we will turn our attention to where the sacrament of reconciliation stands within the society and how it needs to function differently in order to be an agent of healing in this era.

Understanding Addiction

The literature defines addiction as any process over which we are powerless. Addictions take control of us and cause us to do and think things that are inconsistent with our values, evidenced by a sudden need to deceive others and ourselves.

Let us take nicotine as an example. Thirty years ago the United States Surgeon General issued the now famous report linking cigarette smoking with lung cancer. Restrictions first on cigarette advertising and then on smoking itself grew. Many major cities and municipalities in the United States now completely ban smoking in public places. Disregarding city regulations to the contrary, occasionally a student at our university will stand in the hallway for a quick cigarette between classes. "Why are you killing yourself?" I have asked on many occasions.

There is an occasional sneer and sometimes a snide remark. More often, although students will acknowledge that they know smoking is bad for them, they say that they cannot stop smoking for any number of reasons. They cannot stop smoking, for example, because there would be no other way for them to relax, or they would gain tons of weight, or they would not be able to study, and their lists go on. Surely you have either heard or given these or similar rationalizations. Statistics reveal that if people have not begun to smoke cigarettes by age twenty-four, only five percent of them will adopt the practice later in life. For this reason, young people are the primary target of the tobacco industry and those who advertise cigarettes.

What the students' responses indicate to me is that Madison Avenue has seduced them. Perhaps because parents, teachers, and churches have not provided them with adequate reasons and appropriate skills for resisting temptation, they have given in to temptation. They have made cigarettes or drugs or sex their god and have been rendered powerless by them. The same applies to any of the other addictions that control people's lives these days.

Psychologists tell us that there are two major categories of addictions: substance addictions and process addictions. Both function essentially the same way and produce the same results. Although anything can become addictive, nothing must. Some substances and processes, of course, are more powerful than others, but none is intractable in its claim on our free will.

Substance addictions are rather obvious. They are the ones we hear about all the time. These are ingestive addictions. They are almost always mood altering and lead to increased physical dependence. Substances that can be abused include alcohol, nicotine, caffeine, and drugs—any drug that is taken for a purpose other than for which it was intended; that is, to alter one's mood or to avoid dealing with one's inner feelings. Nicotine and caffeine, while initially not as deadly as the others, are equally addictive. Food can also be a substance addiction when it becomes a way of avoiding issues or taking responsibility.

Almost any process can become an addictive agent: spending or accumulating money, gambling, relationships, sex, work, exercise, worry, or religion (the quick-fix variety that does not foster thoughtful prayer or meditation). Psychologists now hypothesize that some of those processes might very well lead to a surge in adrenaline and would therefore more accurately qualify as substance addictions. In that case, adrenaline would be the substance to which one is addicted. When jogging, I have experienced the phenomenon known as a "runner's high," and even when I get on a work rampage, I can feel that adrenaline surging through my veins. This inclines me to agree with the hypothesis that many if not all of these processes might indeed be substance addictions.[17] The data on that, however, is not all in, so in this discussion we will continue to approach them as process addictions rather than substance addictions.

While it might appear from the foregoing discussion that addictions fall neatly into separate categories, do not be deceived. Addictions are slippery, slimy creatures. Rarely, for example, is a person addicted to only one substance or process; it is far more common, for example, for an active or recovering alcoholic to be addicted to caffeine or nicotine as well. Similarly, it is common to substitute one addiction for another or to have an addiction change its shape as does a retrovirus and become something even more intransigent.

Characteristics of Addictive Behavior

The literature gives over twenty characteristics of addictive behavior operative in both individuals and in the addicted society.[18] However, since our purpose here is not meant to be exhaustive, we will examine just a few of those characteristics for the principal purpose of seeing how they relate to the shape that sin takes today.

The first characteristic we will examine is *self-centeredness*. In the addicted society, self is central, while in the gospel society, or church community, relationships are to be central. People become addicted to substances or processes because they like and welcome the sensations that "intoxication" offers them. Consciously or unconsciously, addicts focus their attention on replicating those sensations. According to Stanton Peele, "one of the key dynamics in the addiction cycle is the addict's repeated failure to gain exactly the state sought, while still persisting in the addictive behavior."[19] Although we will examine the culture in greater detail in the following chapter, a quick look at advertising reinforces the message that self is central.

Another characteristic is the *illusion of control*. Addictions appear to offer people a sense of power or control by enabling them to block out such negative sensations as pain, discomfort, or fear. Employees who are addicted to work not only receive a surge of adrenaline from their tasks, but they also expect that their work will control the employer's concept of them. In the addicted society, everyone tries to control everyone else. The worse the addiction, the more desperate the need for control. The addicted society is concerned with accountability and blame; the gospel life is concerned with responsibility—literally, the ability to respond. Addiction, however, actually destroys a person's ability to respond.

A third characteristic is *dishonesty* which can grow into ethical deterioration and/or spiritual bankruptcy. As children we were warned of the "tangled web we weave when first we practice to deceive." The web is now indeed quite a tangled one, and we see it woven in many dusty corners of the culture.

At the outset, dishonesty can be quite subtle and seemingly innocent, but now we see signs that it is beginning to infiltrate our entire culture. It has already permeated our political system. From Watergate to Contragate, a new vocabulary of deceit —or mis-speaking or whatever synonym for dishonesty will be coined tomorrow—has emerged. Euphemistic language itself, which has us discuss things in terms more palatable to our sensibilities, is a subtle form of deceit as well. While the Pentagon has no word for peace except reference to a "pre-hostile condition," it calmly labels the neutron bomb a "radiation enhancement weapon." People rather casually lie to avoid paying taxes or getting traffic tickets. On a more personal level, "being nice" is one of the more insidious forms of dishonesty, and we learn to lie to avoid hurting other people's feelings.

Denial, a fourth characteristic, is a major defense mechanism that seems to be used in epidemic proportions in the addicted society today. Defense mechanisms are psychological devices that shield us from what can harm our psyche. They are an automatic internal protection, but as is true of any kind of defense, internal or external, they can be used inappropriately. In coping with trauma, for example, denial is our first line of defense. When we are told that a loved one has died, "No! No!" is our outcry. Only gradually does reality seep into consciousness. We engage in the same process with simpler crises as well. When we lose the car keys, we first shout, "I don't believe it!"—at least to ourselves. Then we begin to cope with trying to find them.

For addicts, denial becomes a way of life. We know alcoholics, for example, who call themselves social drinkers or are convinced that they are not alcoholics because they only drink wine or beer or because they must have ice cubes in their drinks.

That last one is used as a line of defense by those who are convinced that since alcoholics are known to drink anything and everything, they would not need the amenity of ice cubes. Such rationalizations constitute inappropriate uses of denial.

Projection is another form of denial in which, rather than dealing with our feelings or problems, we project them onto others. Obviously, denial is a major characteristic or a major defense mechanism when it wipes out most of what is being discussed in this book, and it wipes out the document that the Committee on Pastoral Research and Practice published and a lot of other things as well. It takes massive work to break down that wall of denial.

The final characteristic that I will apply in this context is *dependency*—relying on others to meet emotional, psychological, intellectual, and spiritual needs. Dependent relationships are actually the norm within the addicted society. It has been said that addicts don't have relationships; they have hostages. True intimacy requires us to be fully alive and whole—a great threat to the addicted society.

In the late 1970s I heard Henri Nouwen speak at Fordham University. He spoke to a packed lecture hall on a steamy spring evening. To illustrate society's understanding of love, he folded his hands together, intertwined the fingers, and clenched them together. It is a clutching model, and as you will notice by experimenting yourself, it allows no room for mobility, growth, change—all those characteristics we associate with life.

A gospel view of love, by contrast, was illustrated by two palms facing each other, upright, with the tips of the fingers leaning to each other. Try it now. You can feel the power and strength of this more positive bond. Yet the other model, which is completely stifling and in reality leaves neither party free, is the model of love we hear about in songs and see dramatized on television and in movies.

An Addicted Society

Dependent, co-dependent, and counter-dependent are all words that have currency today. At root in each is the concept of dependency. Dependency operates on the scarcity model, which presumes that there is not enough of anything to go around. One must have that drink or that cigarette now because it might not be there later. People are even reluctant to compliment someone for a job well done for fear that there might not be enough praise to go around.

Sibling rivalry is regarded as normal in the addicted society, but it is also woven of fibers of scarcity: the idea that parents do not have enough love to go around for all their children. Love is not a scarce commodity. One is not born with X amount of love that can be exhausted or depleted. Parents have enough love for all their children. There is a different kind of love directed to each child, just as in other relationships, but it is not something one runs out of.

In the same way, I can thank a person without running out of thanks, but that is not how the addicted society operates. It postulates that if somebody else gets something, then there is not going to be anything left for me. That is the major reason why we keep the poor poor—because we need to accumulate more and more. You see, as citizens of the addicted society, we have all been formed in the ways of consumption whether we are conscious of this or not.

Victims of a Formation System

I am using the term "formation system" very deliberately, you will observe. It is not a system of indoctrination in which one is taught what to believe or what to say, but a system of formation in which one is taught how to live out what one believes. In the last three decades, the single most transformative element in American society and the principal means of formation for the American public has been the television.

Adults in mid-life transition now were children in the nascent days of television. Their recollections include test patterns as well as Howdy Doody and his Peanut Gallery. While they might be nostalgic about televisions's magical beginnings, a glance at statistics today tells a very different story.

Time spent in front of the television is on the increase. In the average American home today, the television set is in use for more than six hours a day. William O'Malley observes that "before their first day of school, American children have logged more time in front of the television than with all the teachers they will ever have, and seen more carnage and seduction than a life-long veteran of Genghis Khan's army."[20] In the United States, first graders will spend the equivalent of one entire 24-hour day per week watching television—more time than they spend in the classroom. Surveys show that for most Americans, viewing television has become the third most common activity after sleep and work. . . .[21]

For the past twenty-two years, researchers George Gerbner of the University of Pennsylvania Annenberg School of Communication and Nancy Signorelli of the University of Delaware have found, adults and children have been entertained by about sixteen violent acts, including two murders, each evening during prime-time programming. They also discovered that the rate of violence in children's programs is three times the rate in prime-time shows. By the age of eighteen, the average American child has witnessed at least eighteen thousand simulated murders on television.[22] One cannot miss the tragic irony. As Arnold Fege of the national PTA has observed, if we would not protect teachers who taught violence to children, why would we condone children being exposed to a steady diet of violence on television year after year?

Triumph of Technology

One way of explaining this phenomenon is that television has become the agent of a radical change in human consciousness, comparable to the revolutions in communication that occurred with the invention of alphabetic writing and print. Television, once an optional recreational activity, is no longer optional; rather, it has become a necessary component of all life's activities, public and private, and its influence is evident in a thousand different ways. Once limited to the living room, den, or TV room, the television has now invaded our bedrooms and courtrooms.[23] With technology giving us palm-sized televisions now, teachers regularly confiscate them from schoolbags as they once did water pistols.

I use the term "human consciousness" in the manner defined by Walter Ong as "the individual's own sense of presence in and to himself and in and to the world around him."[24] Television has revolutionized education and the world in an even more dramatic way than the invention of the printing press did. It is the most potent educational device ever created, for good or for evil. While it has the potential for drawing us into a world community, it has an even greater potential for mesmerizing us.

Television tells us the meaning of *success* and *value*, and which choices assure fulfillment. Thrift and chastity were once virtues; now greed and lust are. A sordid world of unimagined deviance is opened up for children every afternoon on the talk shows. For many children, this has become their primary formation system. Parents, caught in the web of getting and spending, have too often abdicated their responsibilities as the guardians and primary educators of their children. The soul message is clear: Nothing succeeds like the appearance of success; noteriety outweighs genuine achievement; and success has nothing to do with substance, only with image.[25]

From this shared reality, mediated by television, the myths of a new age are born, nursery and household tales brought up to date.[26] A few years ago *The New York Times* ran a four-part series, "When Trouble Starts Young," on its front page. When a fifteen-year-old, handcuffed to the wall of a Brooklyn police station house after being arrested in the killing of a man who delivered candy bars to the bodegas, was asked why, he said he had robbed the man so that he could buy a pair of Nikes to replace his three-month-old pair. "The sneakers I had was messed up." he said. "I'd walk down the block and people who know me would start laughing."[27]

As I followed that series of articles, most troubling for me was the casualness with which the murders were treated by all the perpetrators. But should this really surprise us when murder is treated so casually on TV? Why did a nation stand stunned when two children in Jonesboro, Arkansas, turned into mass murderers? Haven't we been "forming" youngsters in the ways of mass murder through television and video games without providing them with appropriate skills for thoughtful reflection on such actions?

Ten years ago I watched my nephews and their friends playing war in the backyard. I noticed that shortly after children were killed, they were back in the game again. When I asked how that was possible, one of the children explained that in the game they were dead only for sixty seconds.

If that sounds too exaggerated or simplistic, pay attention to the lead item each night on the evening news. Adults may be able to distinguish between notoriety and genuine achievement, but a child cannot. Children also cannot always articulate the worries and anxieties that get grafted onto their unconscious minds as a result of adult fixation on some of the more lurid elements of the news. While we have the potential to be as great-souled as Mother Teresa or as soulless as a mass murderer, which looks more appealing, more entertaining when it is played out on the television screen?

O'Malley poses an interesting question: "What would be the effect if the media freely imposed a blackout on reporting terrorism, assassinations, and hostage-taking until they were resolved?" To that I add my own wondering: "What if we gave no publicity without genuine achievement?" Surely advertisers would not like it, but wouldn't we be a better people for it?

Most dangerous for society are the false perceptions that television gives us. When it creates the illusion that the worst problems can be solved in an hour's time, how willing will the next generation be to struggle to achieve anything? Compared with the extravagance of television, reality is boring. The media's radical effect on our spirits has been to make the objectively trivial important, and the objectively important trivial.

Immersion in Consumerism

Any cursory reading of the daily newspaper or weekly magazine demonstrates that idolatry is the sin that overwhelms us—personally, communally, and socially. We appear to worship the products of our own hands and have alienated ourselves from one another in competition and in the struggle for possession and profit. Alienated from our own humanness, we have become transformed into the idols we trust, and the compulsion to consume controls us.[28] We are subjected to what Michael Warren calls the "catechesis of the tube," where the "catechesis" of *Dynasty* and *Dallas* present a religion geared to "the ever greater fulfillment of consumer fantasies."[29]

People no longer find pleasure in the integration of body and interiority but look for pleasure (along with love) in all the wrong places.

To define consumerism as I am using the term, I borrow a fifteen-year-old explanation given by a colleague in liturgical studies. Father Christopher Kiesling understood consumerism to refer to a complex consisting of:

—an economic system which places an extremely high value on the incessant production and consumption of material goods and services at an even higher level of physical convenience and comfort;

—an accompanying mentality which assumes that such a system is the best or only one possible; and

—a related tendency or even drive to find fulfillment in providing and consuming these material goods and services.[30]

As a contrast to consumerism, Father Kiesling described two economic systems: one that sought to produce goods and services to satisfy the basic human needs of an ever wider circle of human beings before increasing the level of physical convenience and comfort of a relatively small population; the other a system designed to produce and consume material goods and services with primary concern for conserving natural resources and environment for the needs of future generations.[31]

What Father Kiesling saw wrong with consumerism almost two decades ago was the fact that it entails *incessant* consumption and production of material goods and services. It calls forth activity—the use of objects or services—to the exclusion of everything truly valuable, bombarding our consciousness with goods and services of every conceivable sort, not only in television advertisements but also in shopping malls, in catalogs, and now even on the Home Shopping Network. From the point of view of social justice, human beings

have a need and a right to some contemplation in their lives—
leisure time for enjoyment of nature and art, for reflection on
life's events and goal. Without such time, it is impossible to be
free and fully human.[32]

"The primary addictions in the Addictive System are addiction to powerlessness and non-living, and all secondary addictions lead to these two primary addictions."[33]

We can conclude that the seven deadly sins seem to be built
into the system of the addicted society! We tend to redefine
morality to fit our behavior. Because denial is the major defense mechanism in the addicted society, however, we natu-
rally have a challenge before us to even see these things.

Could this be the reason we so rarely hear preaching on sin
or no longer see the need for going to confession?

Public Confession

It is somewhat ironic that at the very time when there is this
steady decline in the number of people availing themselves of
the discipline of confession in the sacrament of reconciliation,
the airwaves are rife with public confessions. At almost any
hour of the day or night, one can tune in to what are tanta-
mount to public confessions on television. However, talk
shows, as Sharon Hymer notes, "offer a stripped-down, com-
mercialized caricature of confession. Gone is the vital spiritual
aspect, the bond created when only a chosen few hear our
secrets, the soul-to-soul communion in which the confidant
helps us deal with—not simply spill out—our secrets."[34] That
is the precise difference between the addictive pattern of confessing and the spiritual discipline of confessing as part of the
movement toward reconciliation.

"When you confess," Hymer further observes, "it is not
enough to gain insight into the origins of one of your most
carefully kept secrets and then follow that up with blaming
your mother, your father, your dog, or even yourself for the
lack of forward movement in your life. Once you have understood your secret and then looked at it with the important
people in your life through 'new eyes,' you have to be pre-

pared to abandon, accept or transform it."[35] That is the path toward reconciliation, but the path needs to be broken by God's grace and our willingness to take the alternate route. Addicts tread the same ground over and over again; converts use a different road.

One reason we fail to see this, concludes theologian L. Gregory Jones, is the unfortunate situation that "the grammar of Christian forgiveness has been largely co-opted by a therapeutic grammar." The result is that forgiveness is seen in primarily individualistic and privatistic terms. Consequently, we lose sight of the central role confession and forgiveness play in "establishing a way of life—not only with our 'inner' selves but also in our relations with others."[36]

Looking for Sin in All the Wrong Places

No, sin has not disappeared. As will be discussed at greater length in the next chapter, our culture has so medicinalized our conversation about sin as to make it almost unrecognizable. Cornelius Plantigna states that "the newer language of Zion fudges: 'Let us confess our problem with human relational adjustment dynamics, and especially our feebleness in networking.'" The reason for this, he explains, is that "modern consciousness does not encourage moral reproach. . . . Preachers mumble about sin . . . other traditional custodians of moral awareness often ignore, trivialize, or evade it."[37]

On a personal level, sin may seem to have vanished for a time, as other important parts of our lives did, while we made the transition from childhood to adulthood through that desert of adolescence. As adults, however, we will begin to look more objectively at the fabric of our lives, to see those things that separate or distance us from ourselves, from others, and ultimately from God.

In his book *Sin as Addiction*, Patrick McCormick explains that what has shifted is a basic approach to sin.[38] Although he situates this change historically, I think the shift is replicated in the life of every mature Christian. The shift is from a juridical approach to a medicinal approach.

As was mentioned earlier, the names will be different now. Addiction in all shapes and sizes, consumerism, militarism, sexism . . . the list will go on and on. Sin is with us still, and so too is God, who has promised us mercy.

Returning to the definition used at the beginning of this chapter, we can see that if we have become powerless over, or surrendered ourselves to drugs or alcohol or nicotine or work or amassing money or any of the other substances or processes that were enumerated, we have made them GOD. That is idolatry! In it we see a two-way process: turning away from God and turning toward the idol—the new beloved.

Turn away from God? Me? No way! To the degree, though, that we refuse to accept limitations, imperfections, and creatureliness in ourselves, we have turned away from God. Work isn't our salvation; God is. Radiation enhancement weapons will never give us ultimate security; only God will.

The famous paradigm for conversion in the addicted society has spawned a whole host of twelve-step programs, which seem to have been successful as a result of their realistic grasp of the process of conversion, achieved by "working the program." It is not linear but integrative, as we see in the story of Dave developed by Patrick McCormick in his book *Sin as Addiction*.

Dave is a middle-aged businessman who makes some radical changes in his life after his doctor advises him that he needs to reduce both his weight and his blood pressure if he hopes to survive until retirement age. As Dave cuts down on food, alcohol, and nicotine, he begins to step up his exercise as well. Evening walks with his wife lead them to rediscover their relationship first and then to see the worsening condition of their town. Soon Dave finds himself reading up on toxic waste and taking a more active role in civic government.

The point of McCormick's admittedly simplistic story is to point out that "recovery is organic, constantly working toward fuller and fuller integration. It also includes the reconciling of persons, families, and nations, the healing of familial, societal, and ecological wounds, as well as the sinful rift between humanity and God."[39]

No one is already recovered. That won't happen as long as the community of God is still being built. Recovery is life-giving, honest, holistic, God-centered—cause for celebration in the light, not embarrassment in the dark.

The Many Faces of Reconciliation in the Christian Community

Reconciliation has always had many faces, but in our lifetime most of them have been neglected. Even the *Baltimore Catechism* taught that Eucharist was a source of forgiveness for venial sins, but week after week many people continued to confess venial sins anyway. Was it just to be safe, or did it serve as a "quick fix" for our guilt addiction?

With the liturgy in the vernacular, I continue to maintain that the Roman Catholic community now has a much better sense of how Eucharist is (or can be) a sacrament of reconciliation. Each of the ten formulas for the penitential rite that appear in the Sacramentary (1970) concludes with the rubric "the priest says the absolution" followed by the words:

> May almighty God have mercy on us,
> forgive us our sins,
> and bring us to everlasting life.

The Lord's Prayer, the exchange of peace, and the communion rite all have a penitential and reconciliatory thrust to them as well. It should come as no surprise, therefore, that many people today perceive themselves to be reconciled with God and the community through their celebration of Sunday Eucharist. Rather than argue with what people experience, this is a fine opportunity for the Church to build on what is already sacred ground.

The rite of penance, as we have said, was revised by mandate of the Second Vatican Council: "The rite and formulas of Penance are to be revised so that they more clearly express both the nature and effect of the sacrament."[40] The revised rite was available in 1973 and made mandatory on the First Sunday of Lent in 1976. Since then there has been very slow, sometimes non-existent, implementation. Why? The perception seems to be that "the people don't want it." Could that not be an example of projection?

The reality is that the rite of penance puts demands on both confessors and penitents. While these will be discussed more fully in Chapter Five, it bears mention here. In the old system, confessors sat in the shadows, sometimes hour upon hour, hearing the recital of a seemingly endless line of sins or pseudo-sins, to which they might have responded with the same canned penance and mumbled words of absolution. The anonymous penitent could bob into the confessional, recite the same sins each week, firmly intending not to commit them again, receive absolution, leave assured of redemption at least for a little while, and return to life as usual.

Conclusion

Is reconciliation a lived reality? What we ritualize sacramentally is the living human experience of God we have already had. If the human experience has not happened, then the sacramental ritual makes little or no sense; it becomes an empty gesture.

Do we experience reconciliation in the addicted society? There are many questions but few answers. Are conflicts addressed and reconciled, or are they denied before they conveniently blow over? Can we experience reconciliation with God and the Church if we have never known reconciliation with another? Are parents reconciled with their children, or are children expected to learn about reconciliation in a vacuum?

I still believe that we are in a period of evolution, a sure sign of life, not death. At the moment reconciliation is being sought in a whole host of other ways: through spiritual direction, therapy, interpersonal conflict resolution, retreats, and twelve-step programs galore. There are even some good experiences with the rite of penance happening on Christian Awakening, TEC, and Cursillo weekends, as well as in some parishes. We must recognize that while the rites have been revised, many people (including confessors) have not yet been revised.

Among my students and audiences, the most frequently asked question is, "Why confess my sins to a priest?" From God's point of view, there is no reason. From the human point of view, though, we need to see, hear, and feel forgiveness, not just think about it. And in the addicted society that need is most desperate.

Notes

1. Mark Searle, "The Notre Dame Study of Catholic Parish Life," *Worship* 60 (July 1986) 332.

2. Walter Truett Anderson, *Reality Isn't What It Used to Be* (San Francisco: HarperCollins, 1990) 4.

3. Karl Menninger, M.D., *Whatever Became of Sin?* (New York: Hawthorn Books, 1973) 188.

4. *De Trinitate*, XII, 14.

5. See John Francis Kavanaugh, *Following Christ in a Consumer Society* (New York: Orbis Books, 1981) 91–101.

6. Thomas Kuhn, *The Structure of Scientific Revolutions*, 2nd rev. ed. (Chicago: University of Chicago Press, 1970) 111.

7. Wendell Berry, *The Unsettling of America: Culture and Agriculture* (San Francisco: Sierra Club Books, 1977) 7.

8. Ibid., 9–11.

9. Anderson, *Reality Isn't What It Used to Be*, 107.

10. Gregor T. Goethals, *The Electronic Golden Calf: Images, Religion, and the Making of Meaning* (Cambridge, Mass.: Cowley Publications, 1990) 108–109.

11. James Collier, *The Rise of Selfishness in America* (New York: Oxford University Press, 1991) 216–226.

12. *Beyond Therapy, Beyond Science: A New Model for Healing the Whole Person* (San Francisco: HarperCollins, 1992); *When Society Becomes an Addict* (San Francisco: Harper & Row, 1987); *The Addictive Organization*, written with Diane Fassel (San Francisco: Harper & Row, 1988).

13. *Women's Reality* (Minneapolis: Winston Press, 1981).

14. John Bradshaw, *Creating Love: The Next Great Stage of Growth* (New York: Bantam Books, 1992); *Healing the Shame That Binds You* (Deerfield Beach, Fla.: Health Communications, 1988); *Homecoming: Reclaiming and Championing Your Inner Child* (New York: Bantam Books, 1990).

15. Matthew Fox, "Dear Brother Ratzinger," *National Catholic Reporter* (4 November 1988) 1.

16. See Michael H. Crosby, *The Dysfunctional Church: Addiction and Codependency in the Family of Catholicism* (Notre Dame, Ind.: Ave Maria Press, 1991).

42   *Reconciliation in American Society Today*

17. Stephen Covey, for example, in *First Things First: To Live, to Love, to Leave a Legacy* (New York: Simon and Schuster, 1994) 32–43, refers to this as "urgency addiction" and theorizes that the principal addiction could be to adrenaline.

18. See Schaef, *When Society Becomes an Addict,* 86–93.

19. Stanton Peele, *Diseasing of America: Addiction Treatment Out of Control* (Lexington, Mass.: Lexington Books, 1989) 151.

20. William O'Malley, "The Prophets of Narcissism," *The Way* 31 (April 1991) 125.

21. *Television and Behavior,* vol. 2, p. 339, quoted in Jeremy Murray-Brown, "Video Ergo Sum," in Alan M. Olson, Christopher Parr, Debra Parr, eds. *Video Icons and Values* (Albany: State University of New York Press, 1991) 19.

22. Carl M. Cannon, "Honey, I Warped the Kids," *Mother Jones* (July/August 1993).

23. Murray-Brown, "Video Ergo Sum," *Video Icons and Values,* 18–19.

24. Walter J. Ong, *The Presence of the Word* (Minneapolis: University of Minnesota Press, 1981) 18.

25. O'Malley, "The Prophets of Narcissism," 128.

26. Murray-Brown, "Video Ergo Sum," 21.

27. Celia W. Dugger, "A Boy in Search of Respect Discovers How to Kill," *The New York Times* (May 15, 1994) 1.

28. John Kavanaugh, *Following Christ in a Consumer Society* (Maryknoll, N.Y.: Orbis Books, 1981) 11.

29. Michael Warren, *Faith, Culture, and the Worshiping Community: Shaping the Practice of the Local Church* (New York: Paulist Press, 1989) 123.

30. Christopher Kiesling, "Liturgy and Consumerism," *Worship,* vol. 52, no. 4 (July 1978) 359.

31. Ibid.

32. Ibid., 360.

33. Schaef, *When Society Becomes an Addict,* 15.

34. Sharon Hymer, *Consuming Confessions: The Quest for Self-Discovery, Intimacy, and Redemption* (Center City, Minn.: Hazelden, 1996) 2.

35. Ibid., 19.

36. L. Gregory Jones, *Embodying Forgiveness: A Theological Analysis* (Grand Rapids, Mich.: Eerdmans, 1995) 39.

37. Cornelius Plantinga, Jr., *Not the Way It's Supposed to Be: A Brievary of Sin* (Grand Rapids, Mich.: Eerdmans, 1995) x.

38. See Patrick McCormick, *Sin as Addiction* (Mahwah, N.J.: Paulist Press, 1989).

39. Ibid., 183–186.

40. Constitution on the Sacred Liturgy, no. 72.

Chapter 3

Reconciliation in Sacred Scripture

Go and learn what this means,
"I desire mercy, not sacrifice."
For I have come to call not the righteous but sinners.
(Matt 9:13)

A puzzling silence has replaced the moralizing tone that once characterized preaching about sin. The much-anthologized sermon of Jonathan Edwards, while an example of the extreme, is characteristic of the spirituality that predominated in the not too distant past and affected many people until the present day:

> Your wickedness makes you as it were heavy as lead, and to tend downwards with great weight and pressure towards hell; and if God should let you go, you would immediately sink and swiftly descend and plunge into the bottomless gulf, and your healthy constitution, and your own care and prudence, and best contrivance, and all your righteousness, would have no more influence to uphold you and keep you out of hell, than a spider's web would have to stop a falling rock.[1]

The puzzling silence might give some people cause to sigh in relief, especially if their religious formation was similar to my own, but there is also reason to regret this seemingly fortuitous turn as well.

A frightful fear of damnation was incubated in me as a child. I was quite certain that I would go to hell. As a result, I was very assiduous about religious practices that might get me a reprieve. First Fridays, First Saturdays, rosaries, avoiding cracks in the sidewalk—somehow they all got jumbled up in my head. There was no particular reason for me to feel this way, apart from the generalized myth of unworthiness that lurked beneath everything we were taught about religion in those days. Particularly vivid were those scenes of hell played out for the children of Fatima. If I had been a prankster, my fears might have made more sense, but much as I hate to admit it now, prior to the slump of adolescence I was more like the "goody two-shoes" who almost always did her homework, kept quiet, aimed to please, and got good grades.

Although I will be the first to admit that this preoccupation of mine was unhealthy and unnecessary, I find today's silence equally unsettling. Perhaps the silence results from our reluctance to do unto future generations what was done unto us. Some would say that one source of the impoverished sense of self-esteem that seems almost endemic in American society today[2] is this pervasive feeling of unworthiness learned along with reading, writing, and arithmetic in the Catholic school.

Consequently, with the sole exception of abortion, we seem to steer clear of anything with a moralizing tone and avoid the subject of sin completely. Rarely is the subject approached in a homily, and even on a Sunday when the Scripture passages fairly shriek out the message, the homilist will often take refuge in the second reading or in more generic pious platitudes.

Silence is no more a solution to the problem than denial is. It inevitably leads to confusion and increased unease. The result is that we either get lost in questioning what sin is today, or we give in to over-rationalizing and define sin so narrowly that it is virtually impossible for us to be guilty of it.

On those rare occasions when sin is discussed, instead of sermons on the seven deadly sins and the Ten Commandments, the focus has shifted to the sins of racism, sexism, militarism, and consumerism. Sin, as it has been noted by many, has moved from the bedroom into the boardroom. I am by no means implying that this shift in itself is a bad thing. We were too obsessed with personal unworthiness and needed to be relieved of that sense if we were to survive as whole and holy. It may be, however, that we have gone too far in the other direction.

As we explored in previous chapters, there has obviously been a shift in our sense of sin. What is at risk, however, is not sin but our ability to grasp and say something articulate about the presence of sin in our individual lives and in the world around us. In order to do that, we must return to our roots as a religious people and see how those concepts developed through the Scriptures.

As the noted Scripture scholar Sandra Schneiders has observed, the Scriptures can be read "primarily for information or in view of transformation, that is, to be intellectually enlightened or to be personally converted."[3] While not identical, these two approaches are related. My purpose in this chapter is ultimately transformation: correcting, if necessary, or at the very least developing our understanding and appreciation of sin and reconciliation by seeing how it is treated in the Scriptures. What follows, however, is not a detailed analysis of the Old and New Testaments but rather an overview, with close-ups of two central figures in each Testament: David, Hosea, the prodigal son, and the woman at the well.

Hebrew Scriptures

While there is no one understanding of sin found in the Hebrew Scriptures, it is possible for us to say that there are a few things that have always been true about the different approaches to sin which we find there but which have not been adequately developed or integrated into either our spirituality or catechesis on sin: sin is always linked to a relationship with God and is seen to be unholy; preaching about sin has always been carried out by sinners; and sin is but a shadow of grace.[4] We will return to each of these concepts later in the text.

We must also take into consideration the linguistic structure of the Hebrew language. There is no one word in that language which encompasses an accurate theological understanding of the term "sin." Instead, we find several words and metaphors used which, when taken together, fill out the concept of sin while also helping us to nuance our use and understanding of the term better.

Words and Metaphors

Hattah is the term most commonly translated as "sin." Literally it means "to miss the mark." It did not refer to missing the target in a dart game but to failing to meet an obligation or neglecting a duty owed someone. In the theological sense, this would refer to failure to be faithful to one's duty to the covenant.

Awon, which refers to the state of being twisted, crooked, or bent, encompasses the distortion that remains as a result of sin. This is the burden that is too heavy for the sinner to carry, the mark engraved on the sinner's heart like an inscription in stone, like rust that eats away at metal. In these metaphors we see how our ancestors in faith understood the lasting and pernicious effect of sin. Contemporary metaphors might similarly link *awon* with a virus for which there is no known cure.

A third word that is often translated as "sin" is the Hebrew word *pesha,* which literally means "rebellion." While it more properly refers to political rebellion, it is also applied to rebellion against Yahweh. The demands of the covenant were quite clear: "You will be my people and I will be your God." Time and again, however, the people violated the covenant, that special relationship, choosing instead to serve other gods.

All three concepts address some component of the relationship between God and Israel or between God and an individual. Awakening to the reality of being separated from God usually came as result of encountering God either directly or through the preaching of one of the prophets. Only then did the sinner recognize having violated the sacred dimension of community life.

Origin of Sin

Discussing the origin of sin transports us immediately back to the Garden of Eden. The story of Adam and Eve, however, serves only as an introduction to the concept of sin in the Scriptures. Recall that it was followed in the succeeding chapters of the Book of Genesis by a sweeping display of how sin corrupts. The first sin was followed by first murder, the invention of weapons, and eventually resolute wickedness, resulting in punishment by the great deluge. Although one would expect that humankind had learned the lesson in that cycle, the race that arose thereafter was no different. Instead, it fell into intoxication, unnatural vice, and pride. Again punishment followed, this time in the collapse of the tower of Babel.

The Hebrew Scriptures present us with a panorama of wickedness that is vast and impressive, appropriately and repeatedly setting the stage for the saving acts of Yahweh that follow. Although it is critical not to isolate the story of Adam and Eve from this panorama, it is equally important for us to focus on the mythic dimensions of the story in order to restore its power to our lives.

The Garden of Eden

The story of Adam and Eve was one of the first Bible stories I learned, and I expect that that is true for most people in both the Jewish and Christian communities. Each semester when we begin the "sin" unit in my university courses, I ask the students where evil originated. Inevitably someone answers immediately that it began in the Garden of Eden. I then ask them to tell me the story. At best, what they recount is an abridgement of the story; at worst, a corruption.

It is not the students' ignorance that is responsible for this, but the fact that our culture has robbed us of our myths by rationalizing, literalizing, and consequently trivializing the world's eternal truths and unfathomable mysteries. So I take them, and you, back to the pages of the Book of Genesis. I invite you to read the account in Genesis 2:8–3:24 with your more playful, "right-brain" self. Leave the "left-brain" questions and concerns about accuracy, patriarchy, and anthropology and enter the domain of the primitive right brain. Let the words paint the picture and escort you into that magnificent garden, where every luscious plant you have ever smelled, seen, or imagined grows. Pause, enjoy the garden, sit under your favorite tree, listen to the birds sing, see the sun dancing on the waters before the rest of the story unfolds.

You have it all. Life is on the upswing when suddenly something happens or someone intrudes, dangling something else before your eyes, tantalizing you. In Genesis the temptation came in the shape of a serpent, "more crafty than any other wild animal" that God had made. When the woman told the serpent that God said they would die if they so much as even touched the tree in the middle of the garden, the serpent replied, "You will not die; for God knows that when you eat of it your eyes will be opened, and you will be like God, knowing good and evil" (Gen 3:4-5). The temptation for Adam and Eve was, as it is for us, to be like gods.

Did they need to be gods? Hardly! They had it all, we are told, but if they were made of human fabric, they probably did not realize it at the time. So they gave it all away, choosing instead to be gods, knowing good and evil.

I remember as a child being quite irate with Adam and Eve. I held them directly responsible for all the hardships of my young life, with homework heading the list. Only in time have I come to wrestle with the mystery that is inherent in their choice. At the Easter Vigil, the defining celebration of the Christian people, we sing of their sin as that "happy fault." Had they not sinned, Christ would not have come. "What good would life have been for us?" the *Exsultet* shouts.

In a similar vein, the poet Edwin Muir sees the two worlds in tension in his poem "One Foot in Eden":

> One foot in Eden still, I stand
> And look across the other land.

He surveys the land and "time's handiworks," observing that

> Evil and good stand thick around
> In the fields of charity and sin
> Where we shall lead our harvest in.

Gradually the realization dawns and with it the question:

> What had Eden ever to say
> Of hope and faith and pity and love
> Until was buried all its day
> And memory found its treasure trove?

Concluding that:

> Strange blessings never in paradise
> Fall from these beclouded skies.[5]

As was stated before, it is important for us to tap into the mythic dimension of the story of Adam and Eve in order for it to have any relevance for us today. Too often we get lost in those left-brain questions and concerns about accuracy, patriarchy, and anthropology that I asked you to leave aside for the moment. Myth requires us to enter again that long-neglected domain of the right brain.

Myths, as both Joseph Campbell[6] and Rollo May[7] remind us, are essential to our humanity. Without myths we have no accurate sense of who we are. Myths transcend time. They are about eternal rather than empirical truths. In some way, myth is always true. As May writes, "Myths are essential to the process of keeping our souls alive and bringing us new meaning in a difficult and often meaningless world."[8] And Lillian Feder writes, "It [myth] is a projection in concrete and dramatic form of fears and desires undiscoverable and inexpressible in any other way."[9]

The mythic dimension of the story of Adam and Eve is more about us than about them. Like them, we choose to be gods again and again rather than trusting in the God who made us and longs to be in relationship with us. "Myth is the garment of mystery," wrote Thomas Mann in the preface to *Joseph and His Brothers*, his study of ancient myths,[10] and therefore in order for us to interpret the mythic dimensions of this story for our time, we must look beyond the myth to the mystery. Clothed in the garments of Adam and Eve and their story, we find not their transgression, but their enduring relationship with God. After cataloging for them the penalties resulting from their choice, Scripture says that "the Lord God made garments of skins for the man and for his wife, and clothed them" (Gen 3:21). "In the moments when eternity breaks into time," May writes, "there we find myth. Myth . . . is of the earth in our day-to-day experience, and is a reaching beyond our mundane existence. It gives us the capacity to live in the spirit."[11]

The mythic dimensions of the Garden of Eden remind us that our relationship with God transcends our repeated attempts to be gods ourselves.

God knows we are this way.

> Week after week Christ washes the disciples' dirty feet, handles their very toes, and repeats, It is all right— believe it or not—to be people. Who can believe it?[12]

The Story of David

There is probably no figure in the Hebrew Scripture who commands more attention and respect than King David. Remembered as the faithful servant of Yahweh who slew the giant Goliath with five smooth stones, renowned as the leader of armies to whom the Lord gave victory wherever he went, and cited as the author of the Book of Psalms, David was still human and as prey to temptation as anyone else.

The account of David's great sin is found in 2 Samuel 11:1–12:24. When his troops went out to battle in the spring of the year, David chose to remain in Jerusalem. One afternoon while strolling about on his roof, he saw a very beautiful woman bathing. Instead of dismissing the temptation, David set about discovering her identity. When he learned that she was Bathsheba, the wife of Uriah the Hittite, who was one of his soldiers, he sent for her and "lay with her." When Bathsheba found out that she was pregnant from this liaison, she informed the king. Rather than accepting his responsibility, David contrived a devious plot. On the pretext of gaining information about the war, David sent for Uriah, hoping that while he was back from the front, Uriah would spend the night with his wife, have sexual intercourse with her, and legitimate the pregnancy. Uriah, however, was unwilling to pleasure himself while his comrades were sleeping in open fields.

Obviously, this did not please King David, so he tried another tactic. The next evening he got Uriah drunk, expecting that when inebriated Uriah would not be so principled. But still Uriah would not go to his house.

Finally, in exasperation, David sent a message with Uriah back to Joab, the commander in chief of his army. In it he gave explicit instructions that Uriah was to be stationed in the forefront, where the fighting was worst, and that Joab was to withdraw the other men so that Uriah would be killed.

Joab followed these instructions, and among the battle casualties that day was Uriah the Hittite. After a period of mourning, Bathsheba became David's wife and bore him a son.

To say the least, God was not pleased with David's actions and sent the prophet Nathan to confront him. When they met, Nathan related a story to David that was analogous to his actions with Uriah and Bathsheba. In it he told of two men, one rich and the other poor. While the rich man had many flocks and herds, the poor man had only a small ewe that was kept like a pet in the household. When a guest arrived, the rich man was reluctant to take a lamb from his own flock to prepare for food, so he slaughtered the poor man's lamb.

Enraged at the actions of the rich man, David interrupted the story. Nathan said only, "You are the man!" and later went on to describe the punishment that lay ahead for David: "Thus says the Lord: I will raise up trouble against you from within your own house; and I will take your wives before your eyes, and give them to your neighbor, and he shall lie with your wives in the sight of this very sun. For you did it secretly; but I will do this thing before all Israel and before the sun" (2 Sam 12:11-12).

Remorsefully, David acknowledged his sin and Nathan added, "Now the Lord has put away your sin; you shall not die" (2 Sam 12:13). Because David's deed had shown scorn for the Lord, however, the child born of that illicit union would die. After lying ill for seven days, during which David lay on the ground, fasted, and prayed, hoping that the Lord would have pity, the child died. David rose from the ground, washed, anointed himself, and went to worship before returning home to console Bathsheba.

Notice two things about the story: the Lord sent Nathan to David before David realized the gravity of his offense; and the message from Nathan, "The Lord has put away your sin." In both instances we see the Lord taking the initiative. The Lord still exacts a punishment, but the sin is forgiven.

The Prophecy of Hosea

One could say that the entire prophecy of Hosea is an extended metaphor about sin and forgiveness. It operates on two different levels—Hosea's marriage and his message—which cross and interwine along with God's judgment and mercy throughout the book. Like all the prophets, Hosea spoke within the cultural, political, social, and religious context of his time. He was a voice of God crying in the wilderness of Israel's degradation, and in his tragic marriage he dramatically demonstrated God's redemptive love for humankind.[13]

Apart from this book, we do not know anything at all about Hosea, because he is not mentioned in any other book of the Hebrew Scriptures. He was a prophet in Samaria whose ministry spanned the years between 750 and 725 B.C.E. and a contemporary of Micah and Isaiah, who were prophesying at the same time in the south in and around Jerusalem. Hosea took the place of Amos, preaching the word of God in the north in Samaria.

Hosea's marriage is a story of one-sided love and tells of his obedience to God's command to take Gomer as his wife. "Go, take for yourself a wife of whoredom and have children of whoredom, for the land commits great whoredom by forsaking the Lord" (Hos 1:2). As the story unfolds, Gomer's desertion of her husband and her subsequent reconciliation to Hosea parallel the actions of Israel.

After cataloging the infidelities of Israel, God looks beyond their present waywardness to a future engagement, an eternal betrothal, in which God's faithfulness is matched by Israel's devotion, and a new and lasting relationship is brought about (Hos 2:14-23; 3:5). The tenderness of God's mercy through the prophecy of Hosea is illustrated well by the poetry of Gregory Norbet's song "Hosea":

> The wilderness will lead you
> to your heart where I will speak;
> Integrity and justice
> with tenderness you shall know:
> Long have I waited for your coming home to me
> and living deeply our new life.[14]

The latter part of the Book of Hosea (chapters 4–14) presents a contrast between the corruption and futility of the Israelites' deteriorating relationship with God and the ideal covenant relationship pictured earlier. Within these alternating themes of wrath toward sin and mercy in spite of it, Hosea details the iniquities that shaped the doom of the old relationship and the complete change of direction that must characterize the new. This becomes an analogy for the sinful condition of people of all times—a "diagnosis of the chronic sickness of the human soul and a timeless prescription of love and grace as the remedy."[15]

Hosea was able to speak for God so confidently of forgiveness and reconciliation because God had already spoken to Hosea through his personal experiences with Gomer and her children. As the prophet reflected on his wife's infidelity, God revealed to him the deeper lessons of Israel's unfaithfulness. In seeing Israel's covenant relationship to God as a marriage contract, Hosea was given the perspective by which to judge the defection of his people and the pain it brought to the heart of God.[16]

The sequence of the book is important. After indicting Israel and passing sentence on her, God pledges forgiveness, and Hosea learns from God how to forgive; God takes the lead in restoration, and Hosea follows suit. The first lesson of the Book of Hosea is that we learn forgiveness by being forgiven ourselves, and we learn to accept one who has sinned against us by recalling that we ourselves have been accepted by God. "Forgiveness is the only road to restored fellowship. It clears the air of guilt and despair and brings fresh meaning to life."[17] God takes the initiative in forgiveness, and so too must God's followers.

Summary

Returning to our earlier discussion of the various meanings of sin, in the Hebrew Scriptures sin arises from a deliberate refusal to know God. The prophets presumed that human beings could change their way of life if they wanted to, but they also realized that people do not want to do so. Even the greatest of the prophets probably never anticipated that any more than a small remnant would ever turn back to God.

When we look back to Eden from this perspective, a new question presents itself: Did God throw Adam and Eve out of the garden, or did they throw God out? As we turn now to the Christian Scriptures, we hear that same prophetic cry echoing through the centuries: "Prepare the way of the Lord, make his paths straight"(Mark 1:3).

The Christian Scriptures

When we compare the dynamic of sin, forgiveness, and reconciliation in the Christian Scriptures with what we have just examined in the Hebrew Scriptures, we immediately see a contrast. Whereas in the Hebrew Scriptures forgiveness is a promise, in Jesus that promise becomes a living reality. Forgiveness walks, talks, and embraces the sinner! The term "forgiveness of sins," which we take so blithely for granted in our often-mumbled prayers, is not even found in the Septuagint. With the coming of Jesus, what we have is a completely new and specifically Christian concept, which might help to explain why some found Jesus' message to be blasphemous rather than liberating.

For the Scribes and Pharisees the questions abounded: "Why does this fellow speak in this way? It is blasphemy! Who can forgive sins but God alone?" (Mark 2:7). They were thrown into utter confusion because the power that Jesus claimed for himself in Mark 2:10 exceeded everything the Hebrew Scriptures and Judaism expected from the Messiah. Contrary to their expectations, Jesus came forward as one who both spoke for and acted on behalf of God, making forgiveness, this historical stumbling block, central to the Christian Scriptures.

There is another surprising area of contrast that bears some attention and consideration as well. In the Hebrew Scriptures, some type of punishment always seems to be meted out following sin. If you think back to the story of David and Bathsheba, which we discussed earlier, the penalty exacted was the death of their child, as told in 2 Samuel 12:15-23. Sin is followed by punishment; the pattern occurs repeatedly in the Hebrew Scriptures. God relents but does not appear to forgive until Jesus enters into our story. With Jesus we do not see the same pattern, for he neither exacts punishment from the sinner nor makes it a condition for forgiveness. In fact, this marks a crucial difference between Jesus and the Judaism of his time. Jesus was willing to forgive in God's name without making repentance a prerequisite. Furthermore, he authorized the disciples to do the same.[18]

As we did with the Hebrew Scriptures, we will limit our attention to two famous sinners in order to be able to mine their stories sufficiently. Like David and Hosea, the prodigal son and the Samaritan woman occupy premier places both in salvation history and literature.

The Prodigal Son[19]

We begin our discussion on the Christian Scriptures with the story of the prodigal son, a parable told by Jesus and recounted only in the Gospel of Luke (15:11-32). The context for this parable is the very point we were discussing in relation to the contrast found between the Hebrew and Christian Scriptures: ". . . all the tax collectors and sinners were coming near to listen to him. And the Pharisees and the scribes were grumbling saying, 'This fellow welcomes sinners and eats with them.' So he told them this parable . . ." (Luke 15:1-3). What follows is actually three parables: the lost sheep, the lost coin, and the prodigal son.

Although the story of the prodigal son is probably familiar to you, pay attention to details that might have escaped you in previous readings and to those that strike a chord deep within you.

A man had two sons, and when the younger son asked for his share of the property, the father divided it between them. A few days later, the son "gathered all that he had and traveled to a distant country where he squandered the property in dissolute living." Subsequently a famine struck that country, and when he found himself wanting, "he hired himself out to one of the citizens of that country, who sent him to his fields to feed the pigs." Hungering and neglected, the young man found himself actually yearning to eat the food the pigs were eating. "But when he came to himself," he realized that not only did his father's hired hands have enough bread to eat, but they actually had it to spare, while he was starving to death. Therefore, he resolved to go to his father and say, "Father, I have sinned against heaven and before you; I am no longer worthy to be called your son; treat me like one of your hired hands."

He set off for home, "but while he was still far off, his father saw him and was filled with compassion." The father "ran . . . put his arms around him and kissed him."

The son only managed to get out the first part of his "confession" before the father called for a robe, a ring, and sandals to clothe his son, and for the fatted calf to be killed for the celebration.

When I try to visualize that turning point in the younger son's life, I picture a long, hot day and the young man bent under toil and about to pass out from heat prostration and near starvation. In that half-dazed state, near collapse, he catches a glimpse of his father's hired hands faring much better than he is. It is that picture that enables him to "come to himself" and eventually head for home.

At first reading it is easy to overlook the simple expression "he came to himself," but if you consider the opposite, perhaps some of the dynamism of the expression will return. Have you ever been "beside yourself"? It is an idiomatic expression we use without much consideration of what it actually means. Perhaps you have been beside yourself with worry or grief or frustration. It is a profoundly disorienting experience. We do not decide to be beside ourselves; rather, it is a condition that seems to sneak up on us. Realizing that we are beside ourselves is the first step back into ourselves, enabling us once again to become centered in our self and in God.

As I continue to imagine the scene, I see the young man rehearsing to himself what he will say to his father. On the long journey back home, it becomes a mantra that marks the pulse of his heart and the pace of his gait. The scene, however, does not play out as he expects. "While he was still far off," Scripture says, the father saw him and was filled with compassion. The only way the father could see the son "while he was still far off" was if day by day he scanned the far horizon, hoping and praying for his son's return. That is the image of God that Jesus paints for me in this parable: a compassionate God who yearns for communion with us, luring us with his longing.

God's compassion does not require our confession. God reads our hearts and then leads with forgiveness. Jesus' stories of forgiveness do not require penance either. It is clear that sinners must live with the consequences of their actions, but in the Christian Scriptures we see neither punishment nor penance being exacted as in the Hebrew Scriptures.

An Encounter

The famous story of the Samaritan woman is told in John 4:1-42. In the heat of the day, a woman went to draw water at the well in Sychar. Most women did these heavy chores in the early morning, but their cruel, debasing gossip and their cold, heartless stares made this woman, whose reputation was questionable at best, feel very uncomfortable. So she took to doing her chores when everyone else was indoors.

A man, obviously a Jewish traveler, sat by the well that day and asked her for a drink of water. Such a request was highly unusual, because Jews and Samaritans never spoke to each other. The Jews regarded the Samaritans as a decadent people and, in order to protect themselves from falling into similar sinful ways, the Jews simply never spoke to them. Therefore, to have the Jewish person, let alone a man, make the advance, was most surprising.

When she questioned his asking for a drink of water when he didn't even have a bucket, the mysterious stranger began to talk about living water: ". . . those who drink of the water that I will give them will never be thirsty. The water that I will give will become in them a spring of water gushing up to eternal life" (John 4:14).

If you had to trudge out to the well all the time, such a permanent thirst-quencher would seem very appealing to you.

That wasn't exactly what the man had in mind, however, as the woman could tell from the look on his face. He seemed to be speaking in riddles, and that captivated her. When he asked her to go to get her husband, she admitted that the man with whom she was living was not her husband. Somehow the stranger already seemed to know not only that but also the fact that she had had five husbands before him. That is when she began to think that this mysterious stranger must be a prophet of some sort, and at that very minute Jesus told her that he was the Messiah.

At that point his friends returned, surprised to find him talking with the woman. While they urged him to have something to eat, the woman ran back to town to tell the people what had happened: "Come and see a man who told me everything I have ever done! He cannot be the Messiah, can he?" (John 4:29).

A week . . . a month . . . a year later she probably looked back, knowing quietly within her heart, "Something has happened, something new." The Lord chose to reveal himself to her, and that changed her life. Some of the townspeople joined her, but what about those who did not follow? Perhaps her family and her closest friends stayed behind. There's always another side to such radical changes.

It is not an easy thing to venture out into the uncharted territory virtually alone, to leave behind familiar surroundings for the unknown. Often it seems as though it would be easier to deny the experience we have had and to go back to our old way of living. It might be more comfortable for a while, but would it stay that way for long? The Samaritan woman probably could have gone back to her old ways after her encounter with the Lord, but for how long could she hide from those nagging feelings that come with the knowledge that something indeed had happened, something that made all the difference? The time would eventually come for turning around.

Turning Around . . . Again and Again

That moment of change is what we call conversion—a turning around. It is not a once-and-for-all change, by any means, but rather conversion becomes a way of life in which we are continually called to re-examine our lives and our commitment to the Gospel. Conversions, of course, are not all exactly the same either. Religious conversion, for example, is more deeply rooted in the heart of a person than is the conversion from cigarette smoking. Nevertheless, the geography of conversion in general is somewhat the same.

Our lives, in fact, are dappled with conversions, most of a momentary nature. The fad-diet industry has flourished on the wishy-washy nature of our "conversions." Giving up cigarettes becomes a weekly event for some people, while others continue attempting to live a caffeine-free life. While our intentions are often well motivated, we fall prey to every new craze that comes along.

Why are our conversions so fleeting? Possibly it is because we are not truly convinced of our decision. At the moment it might seem to be a good idea, but when the reality of day-to-day living intrudes, our convictions are tested to their limits, and we are found wanting.

It is no easy matter to break away from any addiction, as the current crop of self-help books demonstrates. In order to break the nicotine addiction, one must be truly convinced that smoking is a major contributor to heart disease and cancer, and that smoking a cigarette is like holding a metaphorical gun to one's head. Both of these convictions are necessary, for I might believe that smoking causes cancer while still harboring delusions that I am eternally immune from the disease.

With weak convictions we fall victim to whoever might happen along the way with a tantalizing offer, for society itself seems to militate against supporting us in any kind of conversion whatsoever. That is precisely why those groups that form around the needs of individuals are so successful. Alcoholics Anonymous, for example, doesn't offer a miracle cure for the disease of alcoholism; what it does offer is a support group— a community of persons who are at various stages in their struggle with the very same disease. Together people find strength in confronting the negative pull of society. They realize that their lives have become unmanageable and expect that there will be difficulty in overcoming their addiction.

Lessons Learned

Just as we have seen that sin is always linked to a relationship with God, so too are forgiveness and living a reconciled life. The love of God, we have seen, is stronger than any sin, and its power can heal the wounds caused by sin, opening up for us a new and reconciled life. Hence we learn to forgive by realizing that we ourselves have been forgiven. Similarly, we learn to accept those who have sinned against us by recalling that we ourselves have been accepted by God, lured back into relationship by God's gracious initiative and not our own. Finally, we learn to live on, united in God's love, in the reconciled community by taking seriously the meaning of grace in our lives. The community continually recalls this great reconciliation in its celebration of the Eucharist. It is then left for each of us to translate the words of our lips into the deeds of our lives. That is the ministry of reconciliation that has been entrusted to each of us.

Notes

1. Jonathan Edwards, "Sinners in the Hands of an Angry God," in *A Jonathan Edwards Reader,* ed. John E. Smith, Harry S. Stout, and Kenneth P. Minkema (New Haven: Yale University Press, 1995) 96.

2. See Robert Bly, *The Sibling Society* (Reading, Mass.: Addison-Wesley, 1996).

3. Sandra M. Schneiders, *The Revelatory Text: Interpreting the New Testament as Sacred Scripture* (San Francisco: Harper, 1991) 13.

4. Patrick McCormick, *Sin as Addiction* (New York: Paulist Press, 1989) 14.

5. Edwin Muir, "One Foot in Eden," *Collected Poems* (New York: Oxford University Press, 1965) 227.

6. Joseph Campbell, *The Power of Myth* (New York: Doubleday, 1988). See also Lawrence Madden, ed., *The Joseph Campbell Phenomenon: Implications for the Contemporary Church* (Washington, D.C.: Pastoral Press, 1992).

7. See Rollo May, *The Cry for Myth* (New York: Norton, 1991).

8. Ibid., 20.

9. Lillian Feder, *Ancient Myth in Modern Poetry* (Princeton: Princeton University Press, 1971) 28.

10. Thomas Mann, *Joseph and His Brothers,* trans. H. T. Lowe-Porter (New York: Penguin Books, 1978).

11. May, *The Cry for Myth,* 297.

12. Annie Dillard, *Teaching a Stone to Talk: Expeditions and Encounters* (New York: Harper & Row, 1982) 20.

13. David Allan Hubbard, *With Bands of Love: Lessons from the Book of Hosea* (Grand Rapids, Mich.: Eerdmans, 1968) 9.

14. Gregory Norbet, O.S.B., "Hosea" (Weston, Vt.: The Benedictine Foundation of the State of Vermont, Inc., 1972).

15. Hubbard, *With Bands of Love,* 10.

16. Ibid., 23.

17. Ibid., 61.

18. L. Gregory Jones, *Embodying Forgiveness: A Theological Analysis* (Grand Rapids, Mich.: Eerdmans, 1995) 150.

19. For an extended reflection on this parable, see Henri Nouwen, *The Return of the Prodigal Son: A Meditation on Fathers, Brothers, and Sons* (New York: Doubleday, 1992). See also Edward Villella, *Prodigal Son: Dancing for Balanchine in a World of Pain and Magic* (New York: Simon & Schuster, 1992) 197–211, for an extended reflection on the ballet version of this parable.

Chapter 4

Through the Lens of History

To assume that the Church's practice of sacramental reconciliation was always restricted to or even included private individual confession to a priest is to be completely off target.
Nothing could be further from the truth. Yet this is a common
assumption held by many Catholics today, both those who
continue to seek reconciliation with the Church through this
sacrament and those who reject it as archaic or irrelevant.

The history of the sacrament of reconciliation is as colorful
and variegated as a spring garden. There was no uniform
practice until the Fourth Lateran Council in 1225, and not until
the Council of Trent in 1551 was private individual confession
first mandated as the only orthodox understanding of
penance. You might say it is but one late-blooming species off
in the corner of the garden. To look only at that one plant is to
miss the beauty of the garden and to misjudge its importance
in the life of the garden. While this chapter will examine the
development and practice of that particular form of the ministry of reconciliation, it will do so in the context of history.

Dealing with the history of any sacrament is more easily
said than done. Prior to the Fourth Lateran Council, there was
no uniform discipline on sacraments, so all attempts to make
their historical development read smoothly are futile. Furthermore, because Christianity developed in an era of persecution,
when any hint of association with "the movement" could lead
to one's execution, we do not have reliable original texts or first-
hand evidence of what we now call sacramental practice. Add
to the mix the realization that the earliest Christians were still

living in an era of hopeful expectation of Christ's imminent return—next week . . . by the end of the month . . . surely this year . . . most definitely within their lifetime—they apparently felt no need to keep historical records. That leaves us limping as historians and relying almost exclusively on "anecdotal comments, homiletic exhortations, and the passing references of polemicists"[1] in our task of reconstructing history. Often what we discover is at best a suspicion of what practice in a particular era might have been. As we will see, that usually comes by indirection or admonishment—circumstantial evidence of the weakest sort. So even with using the garden metaphor, there will be some species of penitential practice we cannot name and others we might never notice.

Before we hurl ourselves back in time, let me say a bit more about the garden metaphor being used here. In the Northeast, after we have survived being buffeted by winter's icy winds and long soulfully for the return of the sun, year after year spring seems to catch us off guard by her beauty. Although the hours of daylight gradually begin to stretch and the season has a few false starts, there finally comes the day when we are sure that spring has arrived. The forsythia pop out first, delicately heralding the season. When we notice the magnolias about to bloom, our spirit begins to soar. Soon they are displaced by the riotous azaleas in every color imaginable. As each new flowering tree matures into its lush greenness, another species unfolds, each more precious than the last, it seems. But each is beautiful and important in its own time and in its own right. Together they are a garden of delight.

In the garden of reconciliation we also see many different flowering plants, shrubs, and trees, notice their fragrance and beauty, and come to understand how each fits into the garden. There are, however, some general things we should observe first about the history of sacramental reconciliation to prepare the ground for our discussion:

- As James Dallen has noted, what we call the sacrament of reconciliation has had so many seasons and changed so markedly over time "that it seems only a convention that we regard it as the same sacrament in each era."[2]

- Throughout the centuries of Christian history, all those who have been involved in the legislation about and the ministry of reconciliation have been sinners.

- At the same time, there have always been people whom Christians have recognized as "holy ones" or agents of God, and have been sought out for wisdom and counsel.

- Regardless of how it might have looked, the sacrament of reconciliation has always been about restoring communion between God, the community, and the individual sinner.

- No garden is without weeds!

There have been many fine histories of the sacrament of reconciliation written in recent years,[3] and it is not my intention to duplicate their work. Rather than focus on the minute details of history, I will present the material under the four broad headings that characterize this sacrament's history: first fervor; public penance; monastic influence; integration. We will do this by taking a close-up look at what was happening with the sacrament in the early years of Christianity and then at various intervals. The purpose of studying the history of the sacrament of penance, as Catherine Dooley notes, is not "to restore the past but rather to enrich the present and the future through the interaction of the tradition with contemporary theology and pastoral practice."[4]

First Fervor

Despite what we read in the Scriptures about forgiveness, there is no clear evidence that in the early days of Christianity the Church allowed for a formal ritual reconciliation of those who committed grievous sin after baptism. In fact, the opposite appears to be true. Keep in mind that baptismal practice, as it developed, required a lengthy period of study and preparation known as the catechumenate. Given this preparation, it was not expected that people would stray far from their commitment. It was also a time of persecution for the Church, and therefore maintaining a hard line with regard to repentance and reconciliation was an attempt to strengthen the resolve of its members.

Be careful to note that this refers specifically to "grievous sin"—a total disruption of a person's relationship with the community. Murder, adultery, and apostasy were prime examples and in some particular churches were the last to be considered reconcilable offenses precisely because of the manner in which they violated the covenanted relationship. Lesser offenses of the common life were forgiven in a formal communal setting through the practice of public confession. In the earliest texts we read of their practice:

> At the church meeting you must confess your sins, and not approach prayer with a bad conscience. That is the way of life.[5]

> On every Lord's Day—his special day—come together and break bread and give thanks, first confessing your sins so that your sacrifice may be pure. Anyone at variance with his neighbor must not join you until they are reconciled, lest your sacrifice be defiled.[6]

This is not unlike the practice of mutual confession of faults recorded in the New Testament:

> If we say that we have no sin, we deceive ourselves, and the truth is not in us. If we confess our sins, he who is faithful and just will forgive us our sins and cleanse us from all unrighteousness (1 John 1:8-9).

> Therefore confess your sins to one another, and pray for one another, so that you may be healed (Jas 5:16).

Similarly, it is very much like the various forms of the penitential rite found at the beginning of the Eucharistic celebration today.

Public Penance

Theologically speaking, the first sacrament of penance was actually baptism. The first Christians were initiated into the community as adults, and their sins were washed away in the baptismal pool. It was not expected that they would ever sin again. Over the course of several generations, however, the practice of publicly reconciling penitents gradually developed. Reconciliation in this form was harsh but rare. In practice, it looked like the catechumenate: the bishop in the presence of the community of believers granted forgiveness. Theologically, it was understood to restore the baptismal grace that had been damaged or eaten away by sin. There was, however, no universal practice for reconciling penitents, and the specific ritual varied from one episcopal see to another. Before discussing those various local practices, let us take a look at what might have been a fairly typical case.

The year was about 250 B.C.E. Although Louis came from a devout family, as a young man he fell in with a pagan gang, drawn in by their carefree ways and easy access to high living. Before long he found himself frequenting the local brothel. Although it troubled his conscience at first, as time wore on he found that his visits increased and his concerns decreased to the point that he hardly gave it a second thought. Gradually he began to distance himself from his family and friends. It was almost as though he had moved to a foreign country.

One evening several years later, he was jolted to his senses. In the shadows where he surveyed the local prostitutes, he saw a young woman who closely resembled his younger sister. In a flash, he saw how far he had strayed from all that he once held sacred. No matter how hard he tried, he was unable to dismiss that awareness from his consciousness. Humbly he presented himself to the pastor, confessed his sin, and asked to be received back into the community.

Louis was enrolled in the order of penitents, and each Sunday as the community gathered together for Eucharist, Louis knelt outside the gathering place, asking for the community's prayers and God's forgiveness. As time wore on, his clothing was in tatters. The pattern of his life, though, began to change. Although he was still tempted to stray from his resolve, he relied on the strength of the community and God's help. He recalled the reassuring words of Saint Paul to the community at Corinth: "Three times I appealed to the Lord about this, that it would leave me, but he said to me, 'My grace is sufficient for you, for power is made perfect in weakness'" (2 Cor 12:8-9).

After three years, Louis was welcomed back into the community on Holy Thursday in a celebration similar to the one described by an early historian.

A contemporary account of a service of reconciliation has been left by the historian Hermias Sozomen. Writing in the middle of the fifth century, he portrayed the penitents at a Roman liturgy standing together "with downcast eyes and mournful faces." Then, "wailing and lamenting they throw themselves prostrate on the floor. Looking at them with tears in his eyes, the bishop hurries towards them and likewise falls to the floor. The church echoes with loud cries and the whole congregation is filled with tears. After this the bishop gets up and raises those who are prostrate, and after praying for the penitents in a befitting manner, he dismisses them. Then each one on his own performs the difficult works for as long as the bishop has assigned, either fasting, or not bathing, or abstaining from meat, or doing other things which have been prescribed. When he has paid his penalty like a debt, on the day appointed he is acquitted of his sin and takes his place in the congregation."[7]

Although it might not seem that way to you, Louis was lucky. He was able to be reconciled. Had he been guilty of another sin in that era—apostasy, let's say—he would have had to wait until he was on his deathbed to be reconciled.

Monastic Influence

Crossing the European continent, we next look at penitential practice in sixth-century Ireland, converted through the missionary campaign of the "bishop" we know better as Saint Patrick.[8] As we stand outside Irish society and at a distance of fifteen hundred years, we may consider that their penitential discipline might seem to have been too rigorous to even be taken seriously. However, when we look at their practice alongside Celtic legal procedures of the time, we see how congruent they are to the society that lived with them.[9]

The penitential manuals bequeathed to us show a Church structure that was based on the monastery rather than on the diocese as an ecclesiastical unit. Under the leadership of abbots and learned monks, monasticism flourished in Ireland. Just as the rest of their society was ordered, so too was the monastery, housing monks, clerics, students, and penitents.

The monks had a very definite understanding of the moral life patterned by Jesus Christ, and their concrete views on behavior were consistent with that pattern. To their way of thinking, there were certain diseases of the soul that ruptured one's relationship with God, and restoring that relationship to full spiritual health required suitable penitential exercises. Penitential activities included fasting from food and sleep, repeated genuflections, and praying for long periods of time with arms outstretched in identification with the crucified Christ.

In the Irish monastery, to ensure fidelity to the Christian way of life, each monk or nun was required throughout life to make a regular confession of faults to a spiritual mentor, or *anamchara*, which in Irish means "soul-friend." Lay men and women living in or near the monastery also had recourse to an *anamchara* for spiritual guidance. Originally the *anamchara*'s role was not to serve as a judge but rather as a spiritual companion on life's journey, offering assistance, through dialogue, over the difficult patches of ground. This practice was not initially an official ecclesial act.

Unlike the Latin practice, there was no "order of penitents" within the Celtic system. Forgiveness, therefore, could be sought by anyone. Similarly, there was no public dimension to the process, which consisted exclusively of private penitential exercises usually involving fasting on bread and water together with prayer. Because it was private, persons could avail themselves of this practice without the censure that accompanied the public penance discussed previously. These dire consequences included permanent exclusion from the clergy as well as public office, prohibition of marriage, or abstinence from sexual intercourse for a long period of time. Unlike public penance, which could be received only once, Celtic penance was repeatable, and people were encouraged to avail themselves of its healing powers regularly.

From the sixth century onward, then, on any day of the year, following a confession that could include less serious sins, there existed the possibility of repeated absolution by a priest and not only a bishop. Although the first penances were noted for their severity, in time, through a system of commutation, these were reduced to include financial contributions, the repetition of prayers, self-flagellation, and similar practices.[10]

Era of Integration

In the early sixth century, British and Irish monks joined the missionary effort on the European continent to assist in the recovery from the barbarian invasions. Along with their intentional work of founding monasteries, building churches, and establishing schools in what today we know as France, Spain, Germany, Switzerland, and northern Italy, these monks, probably inadvertently, also implanted their penitential discipline in that part of the world. The result was that for a significant period of time, perhaps as long as six hundred years, both canonical and monastic forms of sacramental reconciliation co-existed on the European continent.

Among the faithful, the new method met with quick acceptance, not because it was an easy way out, but rather, since it could be received more than once, it promised salvation that baptism could no longer assure. Unlike canonical penance, it could also offer forgiveness for less than capital sins, which enabled an increasing number of people to avail themselves of this valuable spiritual discipline. However, we cannot conclude that this practice of private confession was by any means popular. Were that so, it would not have been necessary for legislation regarding its minimal frequency to be developed.

Although to us who know a similar practice it would seem that the appeal of this form of the sacrament should be greeted with rejoicing, such was not the case. Instead, reaction among the European clergy was just the opposite. They made strong attempts to resist its spread, because they regarded this new form as an "unscrupulous cheapening of divine forgiveness" and a violation of the Church's tradition that post-baptismal repentance could be acknowledged only once. The bishops gathered at the Council of Toledo in 589 stated the case forcefully:

> We have learned that, throughout some churches [parishes and/or dioceses] of Spain, the faithful are doing penance not according to the canonical rule but in another detestable way. That is, as many times as it pleases them to sin, they ask a presbyter to grant them pardon.
>
> We want to put an end to such an abominable presumption. [*Therefore,*] this sacred council orders that penances be given according to the rite [*procedure*] prescribed by the ancient canons: that is, that the person who repents of his evil deeds be excluded temporarily from Eucharistic communion and, along with other penitents, ask often for the imposition of hands; and that, when the time of his satisfaction is completed according to the judgment of the bishop, he be readmitted to communion.
>
> Those who relapse into their sins, either while doing penance or after they have been reconciled, must be condemned according to the severity of the ancient canons.[11]

Despite their adamancy, the practice continued, and in 650 a Council in Chalon approved confession to priests as "a medicine for the soul" and "helpful to people."

Although it might seem as we read this discussion that the new method afforded the penitent a quickie confession, such was far from the case. It was the monastic understanding that repentance was not reserved to those who sinned seriously but was an elementary requirement of the gospel. The disciplinary practices they prescribed were intended to reshape the spirit in conformity to Christ. The practice flourished, books multiplied, confessors were cast in the roll of judges, and abuses crept in as well. It was the Fourth Lateran Council in 1215 that finally decreed private confession to be the official sacrament of repentance. However, solemn public penitence and reconciliation remained under the jurisdiction of the bishop for those sins reserved to the bishop for forgiveness.

Scholastic Contribution

The timeless contribution of Scholasticism, primarily in the thought and writings of Saint Thomas Aquinas and Peter Lombard, was that it brought a theological focus to the discussions of the sacraments. Although contemporary theologians might nuance the discussion differently, the theological constructs with which they framed the arguments are still in use today. It is also important to keep in mind that the men who framed this discussion knew only private confession. Consequently, in the continuum of sin to reconciliation, their attention was limited to confession and absolution.

Because not everyone agreed on those issues, it is not possible for us to speak about the Scholastic contribution with a single voice. Rather, the Scholastics' contribution consisted of many voices. Sometimes they were contradictory, and sometimes they seemed to be speaking simultaneously. That is not cause to ignore them, however, but rather to listen to them more carefully in order to hear what they have to say to us today.

The so-called early Scholastics thought that the "power of remitting sins" was to be found in the shame and sorrow felt in the act of confessing. For them, that alone was the effective cause of being released from the sins of one's past. For Peter Abelard, writing in the twelfth century, it was perfect contrition, motivated by the love of God, that effectively removed sins from one's soul. He saw that the priest's absolution referred only to the satisfaction that had to be made for the sins. Peter Lombard, whose *Sentences* was widely known and used in his day, taught that if no priest was available, confession could be made to a lay person to obtain God's forgiveness. He excluded absolution from his definition of the sacrament. For him, the role of the priest was simply to assure penitents that their sins were forgiven, to assign the penance, and perhaps to remit some of the punishment by giving absolution. As if in rebuttal, Hugh and Richard of St. Victor argued that if the priest forgave the punishment, he effectively forgave the sin.

By now it should be obvious that not everyone agreed. Therefore, it should not be surprising that both of these explanations of confession, or more precisely, contrition and absolution, were taught in the schools of Europe at the beginning of the thirteenth century.

It was, in fact, attempts to reconcile these two positions that led to distinctions between mortal and venial sins, perfect and imperfect contrition, and temporal and eternal punishment, which so shaped conversation about the sacrament of penance into the twentieth century. Still the question remained: What is the sacrament of penance? Is it the act of penitent or the action of priest?

Thomas Aquinas provided the answer. It is both! His explanation spoke of the "matter and form" of the sacrament. He agreed with his predecessors that sins can be forgiven by perfect contrition even without a priest's absolution. In fact, Aquinas had more in common with earlier Scholasticism than later writers, like John Duns Scotus, who focused only on absolution.

Churchmen in the later Middle Ages often accepted Aquinas's definition of the sacrament because it covered all the parts of the ritual, but their understanding of its purpose and operation was closer to Scotus's explanation. The sacrament effected the forgiveness of sins, but it ceased to have any noticeable effect on people's lives. The social implications of sin and reconciliation had been long lost, and all that survived was individual private confession to a priest.

Era of Reform

As James Dallen observes, "The introspective individualism of the Renaissance intensified the effects of the mechanical ritual."[12] The spirituality of the day, *devotio moderna*, reflected in the popularity of such works as Thomas à Kempis's *Imitation of Christ*, for example, further exacerbated the situation.

With the exception of Martin Luther, who continued to champion the importance of private confession, the other Reformers rejected the concept of needing a priest to mediate forgiveness, which comes from God alone. This set the stage for the Council of Trent to assert that forgiveness—or more accurately, absolution—could only be obtained by making a complete confession to the priest. The bishops gathered at the Council of Trent did not have the benefit of knowing the historical background just now presented. Neither did they seem to have theological understanding that sin affects one's relationship not just with God but also with the community. They saw only the need to hold the line against the Reformer's incursion on what they regarded to be the undying tradition of the Church.

The Roman Ritual of 1614, therefore, was as spare as possible. "Anything that might distract from the priest's authority and power," Dallen further notes, "was edited out, including references to the penitent being restored to the Church community."[13] Despite some futile attempts to revisit the social character of reconciliation, that is how the situation remained for four hundred years, until the dawn of the Second Vatican Council.

Notes

1. James Dallen, *The Reconciling Community: The Rite of Penance* (New York: Pueblo, 1986) 2.

2. James Dallen and Joseph Favazza, *Removing the Barriers: The Practice of Reconciliation* (Chicago: Liturgy Training Publications, 1991) 5.

3. See James Dallen, *The Reconciling Community*; Monika Hellwig, *Sign of Reconciliation and Conversion: The Sacrament of Penance for Our Times* (Wilmington: Michael Glazier, 1984). A briefer historical treatment of the sacrament can be found in Catherine Dooley, "The History of Penance in the Early Church: Implications for the Future," in *Reconciliation: The Continuing Agenda,* edited by Robert J. Kennedy (Collegeville, Minn.: The Liturgical Press, 1987) 83–95.

4. Dooley, "The History of Penance in the Early Church," 84.

5. *Didache,* 4:14, as found in *Early Christian Fathers,* ed. Cyril C. Richardson (New York: Macmillan, 1971) 173.

6. *Didache,* 14:1-2, ibid., 178.

7. *Ecclesiastical History,* VII, 16.

8. In his *Confessions,* Patrick describes himself as a "bishop" who is a "resident of Ireland," although there is a question among scholars as to whether Ireland in Patrick's time had a centralized ecclesiastical seat.

9. For a more thorough discussion, see Kathleen Hughes, *The Church in Early Irish Society* (Ithaca, N.Y.: Cornell University Press, 1966).

10. To bring fairness and uniformity, over the course of time books of sins with appropriate penances were compiled.

11. *Concilium Toletanum*, III, Capitulum 11; Mansi, *Conciliorum collectio*, vol. 9, col. 995.

12. James Dallen, "The Sacrament of Penance: Historical Perspectives," in Dallen and Favazza, *Removing the Barriers*, 13.

13. Ibid., 15.

Chapter 5

Reconciliation as Sacrament

Crowds pass by reverently. This is sacred ground. There are no rules or regulations about silence posted. One just knows to honor the silence.

They come—young and old, wounded and whole, uniformed and not. They pause and gently, lovingly touch the gleaming marble and the recesses of memory.

The wall seems to answer back, dramatically enabling those who come close to see themselves reflected in the experience and part of the larger reality.

They leave messages, flags, flowers. Some meet fathers they never knew; others touch a grief they never knew they had. It is a holy place.

From its dedication in 1982, the Vietnam Memorial in Washington, D.C., has been a sanctuary of memory. "In its ambience, we could all be moved to forgive one another," writes Mary Collins.[1]

Why? In a culture that is increasingly devoid of reverence for anything—especially for the human person—the reverence shown at the Vietnam Memorial stands in stark contrast.

A similar monument to the ravages of war stands in Coventry, England. As the story goes, the city of Coventry was virtually sacrificed during World War II. In reprisal for the night raids on German cities, the Nazis determined that only the material and psychological destruction of an entire city would be fitting retaliation. Because of its small size (about a quarter million inhabitants), its strategic location in the center of England, and its many aircraft factories, the city of Coventry was chosen.[2] The Allies had managed to break the Nazi code and knew that Coventry would be bombed. To alert the city, however, would mean sacrificing this prime source of information, so it was decided to let the city be sacrificed instead.

On the night of Thursday, November 14, 1940, bombs fell and the city of Coventry suffered the longest air raid of any one night in Great Britain during the entire Second World War. Among the casualties was the magnificent fourteenth-century cathedral church of St. Michael. Its outer walls, the tower, and the spire remained intact, but the wooden roof, heavy oak ceiling, pews, floor, and screen were completely destroyed.

Although at the time this seemed to be the end of the city's magnificent cathedral, two precious relics remained that brought new life and purpose out of the destruction. A few days after the bombing, two irregular pieces of the charred roof beams were tied together by wire and set up at the east end of the ruins. This "Charred Cross" stood behind the stone altar in the sanctuary of the ruins, with the words "Father forgive" carved into the wall behind it.[3]

Another relic, the hand-forged nails that had once fastened together the cathedral's beams, littered the ruined floor of the sanctuary, but as the smoke cleared, someone was struck with the inspiration of forming three of the nails into the shape of a cross. As a result, the Cross of Nails has become the symbol of Coventry Cathedral's ministry of international reconciliation.

In 1954, when the time came to rebuild the city's cathedral, the decision was made not to raze the old cathedral but to let it stand as a memorial to the ravages of war. Standing in the shadow of the new Cathedral of Saint Michael, all that remains today of the old cathedral are its walls and an altar that was fashioned from the rubble.

The theme of reconciliation echoes throughout the great cathedral. For forty days and forty nights before the consecration of the new cathedral, the Cross of Nails from the old cathedral was taken on a pilgrimage to every parish in the diocese of Coventry. Only then was it brought to the new cathedral and placed within the center of the high altar cross, where it appears to be nestling in the palm of God's hand.

Both of these memorials speak to a universal need people have for ritual, a way of weaving words, symbols, and actions together that enables them to express the inexpressible. In both of these examples and in countless more, people are able to express and effect what they mean. When the Church does this, we call it "sacramental."

Just as humans need rituals to mark the important thresholds, passages, and experiences of their lives to intensify or effect what they signify, so does the Church, and the most powerful of these are our seven ritual sacraments.

In the Beginning . . .

The Church's understanding of sacrament has been growing through the two thousand years of Christianity. Jesus did not sit the disciples down on the hillside, ask them to take out their notebooks, and begin dictating the list of seven sacraments and how they were to be celebrated. We cannot even find in the Scriptures specific references to the institution of each of the sacraments as directly as we have for the institution of Eucharist: "Do this in memory of me."[4]

The Church has understood that Jesus instituted the sacraments by deeds rather than by words alone. Developing that understanding, however, took over a millennium. In the first ten centuries, in fact, there was no enumeration of the rites we now call "the seven sacraments."[5] To even consider the theological concept of sacrament, as we use the term today, was an anomaly before Peter Lombard in the twelfth century and was not doctrinally defined until the Council of Trent (1545– 1570). This does not mean that there were no sacraments until the Council of Trent called them into being. Sacraments are rooted in the death and resurrection of Jesus—a permanent pledge of God's presence with us, covenanted in Jesus' blood: "I will be with you all days. . . ." Rites change; sacraments do not.

In the last chapter we saw how the Church's ritual approach to reconciliation underwent massive shifts over time. At no time, however, did that affect the sacrament itself—God's merciful embrace of the repentant sinner. God does not need sacraments in order to forgive the sinner, but the Church needs them in order to express and effect that reconciliation, and as Church, we need sacraments to experience the enduring presence of God-with-us, covenanted in Jesus' death and resurrection. Although the seven ritual sacraments are not the only way in which we experience the presence of God-with-us, they are the principal way in which the community of believers expresses and effects its unique relationship to God and with one another.

Sacraments of Reconciliation

Reconciliation has a broader sacramental context than the rite of penance, and our discussion more properly begins with baptism. Although today stress is laid more on the interpersonal nature of original sin as "a deprivation of original holiness and justice,"[6] it is still the concept we use as the point of origin for this sinful, egocentric society in which we live. Through the waters of baptism, which "impart the life of Christ,"[7] whether to infant or adult, we are incorporated into a theocentric community that continually attempts to overcome that sinful orientation of humanity that constitutes original sin.[8]

In the early days of Christianity, those preparing for initiation would spend the forty days of Lent in a kind of spiritual retreat. The focus shifted as they came to this time of spiritual preparation known as the period of enlightenment or illumination. All their previous months or years of preparation had been spent trying to examine the doctrinal and practical aspects of Christianity. Whereas the mind had been primed before, now it was time to prime the heart.

Scrutinies

In addition to the entire season of Lent serving as a dramatic backdrop for the process of conversion, the readings of three Sundays of Lent invite the whole Church to examine three important elements of the Christian life. The Church refers to these celebrations as the "scrutinies" and celebrates them on the Third, Fourth, and Fifth Sundays of Lent. Their purpose is mainly spiritual: "to uncover, then to heal all that is weak, defective, or sinful in the hearts of the elect and to bring out, then to strengthen all that is upright, strong, and good."[9] In other words, these rituals encourage the members of the community to scrutinize themselves and to arouse in the elect in particular "the desire for purification and redemption by Christ."[10]

While the ritual action of each of the scrutinies is identical, their content differs from week to week in relation to the Scripture readings of that day. In each celebration, after the homily, the elect, together with their godparents, come before the celebrant, who asks the community to pray in silence for the elect.

On the Third Sunday of Lent our attention is turned to the Samaritan woman who met Jesus at the well, as narrated in John 4:5-42.

Jesus knows each of us as we are—sinners. Still, he reveals himself to us and invites us to be reborn in the spirit of his love. We want to reject everything in our lives that separates us from Jesus, but this should not lead us to reject ourselves, for we are loved by God as we are now. Denying or ignoring our sinfulness separates us from ourselves, which only further separates us from the God who loves us despite that sinfulness. In this context, the Church prays for the elect:

> God of power,
> you sent your Son to be our Savior.
> Grant that these catechumens,
> who like the woman of Samaria thirst for living water,
> may turn to the Lord as they hear his word
> and acknowledge the sins and weakness that weigh them
> down.
>
> Protect them from vain reliance on self
> and defend them from the power of Satan.
>
> Free them from the spirit of deceit
> so that, admitting the wrong they have done,
> they may attain purity of heart
> and advance on the way to salvation.[11]

The Scripture readings for the Fourth Sunday of Lent focus on the paradox of sight and are found in John 9:1-41. Here we see the interplay between sight and blindness. Jesus, the light of the world, allows us who are willing to believe to see with new eyes. In his light we see ourselves more clearly, our society more critically, and our God less fearfully. And so we pray for the elect (and for ourselves):

> Father of mercy,
> you led the man born blind
> to the kingdom of light
> through the gift of faith in your Son.
>
> Free these elect
> from the false values that surround and blind them.
> Set them firmly in your truth,
> children of the light for ever.[12]

The third scrutiny is celebrated on the Fifth Sunday of Lent, when we once again hear the story of Jesus restoring Lazarus to life (John 11:1-45). In some way each of us is entombed, tightly bound by the wrappings of selfishness, cynicism, or a lack of self-esteem. Faith in the Lord Jesus restores us to life as it did Lazarus and leads us on the way to eternal life, and so we pray:

> Father of life and God not of the dead but of the living,
> you sent your Son to proclaim life,
> to snatch us from the realm of death,
> and to lead us to the resurrection.
>
> Free these elect
> from the death-dealing power of the spirit of evil,
> so that they may bear witness
> to their new life in the risen Christ,
> for he lives and reigns for ever and ever.[13]

Renewing the Promise

Once we have studied the history of the catechumenate and the restoration of that process in the Church today through the Rite of Christian Initiation of Adults, some students express regret that their parents had them baptized as infants. They think they have missed out on an opportunity to express their public commitment to God and the Church, because by the

time they are seated in my classroom, they have already been
fully initiated into the Church. Even when they did not receive
the sacrament of confirmation until their high school years,
they still consider that theirs was not really a "knowing" commitment.

For those of us who have been fully initiated into the Roman
Catholic ecclesial community, the Lent-Easter cycle provides an
annual opportunity to recommit ourselves publicly to the
Church. Lent can be a reprise of the catechumenate for us, and
with Easter we have the opportunity to renew our commitment.

Both at the Easter Vigil and at Easter Sunday Masses, the rite
of the renewal of baptismal promises is repeated after the
homily:

> Dear friends,
> through the paschal mystery
> we have been buried with Christ in baptism,
> so that we may rise with him to a new life.
> Now that we have completed our Lenten observance,
> let us renew the promises we made in baptism
> when we rejected Satan and his works,
> and promised to serve God faithfully
> in his holy Catholic Church.

Then follow specific questions, beginning with those specifically dealing with sin:

> Do you reject sin, so as to live in the freedom of God's
> children?
>
> Do you reject the glamor of evil, and refused to be mas-
> tered by sin?
>
> Do you reject Satan, father of sin and prince of darkness?

Questions incorporating the items of the Creed follow, and
after the concluding prayer the priest sprinkles the people
with water or in some parishes invites people to the baptismal
pool. This corporate renewal, woven into the rituals of adult
initiation and full incorporation into the Roman Catholic com-

munion, is demonstrated powerfully in the video *This Is the Night*.[14]

Coming to the Table

It should not be the least bit surprising to us that down through the centuries Christians principally experienced reconciliation at Eucharist. Just take a look at the people Jesus invited and welcomed to the table: prostitutes, tax collectors, and sinners of all sorts. Nathan Mitchell has called this form of table fellowship "subversive."[15] When Jesus overhears himself being criticized by the Pharisees for this he replies,

> Those who are well have no need of a physician, but those who are sick. Go and learn what this means, "I desire mercy, not sacrifice." For I have come to call not the righteous but sinners (Matt 9:12-13).

Although we are short on details about this table fellowship, we do know that from the beginning the community continued to gather in the name of Jesus, to eat and drink in his memory, and to proclaim the good news of reconciliation.

> All who believed were together and had all things in common; they would sell their possessions and goods and distribute the proceeds to all, as any had need. Day by day, as they spent much time together in the temple, they broke bread at home and ate their food with glad and generous hearts, praising God and having the goodwill of all people (Acts 2:44-47).

As the liturgy of Eucharist began to take on a more clearly defined structure, its connection to reconciliation also became more clearly articulated. Today we find those same themes woven into the Eucharistic liturgy each time it is celebrated. To borrow a concept from music, reconciliation is a motif that is heard repeatedly in every celebration of Eucharist. The full motif is heard at least five times:

At the beginning of the celebration, turning our thoughts to whom we have pledged ourselves to be as followers of Christ, in either the *Asperges* or the penitential rite we admit our sinfulness and need for God's forgiveness.

In the Lord's Prayer we plead "forgive us our sins as we forgive those who trespass against us."

Before approaching the altar to receive holy communion, following that ritual deep in our ancestral past, we turn to one another in an embrace of reconciliation, restoring the peace that Jesus came to earth to effect.

Then, together in one large chorus, we plead for mercy: "Lamb of God, you take away the sins of the world, have mercy on us."

Finally, as the communion procession is about to form, we make a passionate plea: "Lord, I am not worthy to receive you. Speak but the word and my soul shall be healed."

If our minds and hearts were joined in giving voice to those words, there would be no question about reconciliation being a theme of every Eucharist.

Eucharistic Prayers of Reconciliation

At some celebrations of the Eucharist, prompted by the liturgical texts or season, there is a particular focus on reconciliation. For these the presider might choose to use one of the Eucharistic Prayers for Masses of Reconciliation. Intended for use during the 1975 Holy Year, these prayers were composed at the initiative of the Congregation for Divine Worship. During the Holy Year an attempt was made to draw the attention of the Roman Catholic community in particular to the need for continual renewal and reconciliation. In announcing the theme of the Holy Year, Pope Paul VI pointed to the signs of disunity and alienation that existed throughout the world. The passing years obviously have not obliterated those signs of disunity and alienation. If anything, ours is an age that stands in even more desperate need of reconciliation, yet we have not even begun to pray as we ought.

Unfortunately, because of lengthy negotiations for approval from the Congregation for the Doctrine of the Faith, the Eucharistic Prayers of Reconciliation were not available for use until the celebration of the Holy Year was almost concluded.[16] When they were finally approved by the Holy Father on October 26, 1974, copies were sent to the episcopal conferences that had requested them, and the conferences were directed to choose one for use.[17]

Requests poured in from almost every country, and the new Eucharistic Prayers came into experimental use for a period of time initially ending in 1977 but later extended to 1980. Eventually the prayers were approved indefinitely and were allowed to be published in future editions of the Sacramentary.[18]

The Eucharistic Prayers for Masses of Reconciliation offer the community a powerful means of intercession for ourselves, each other, and the entire world. As Bernard Häring reminded us:

> The Eucharist can bring about the great change: the wonderful consecration of all earthly reality. If we so celebrate the Eucharist that it becomes the form and norm of our life, we discover the beautiful nature of the bread, the wine, of our liberty, our individuality, and of all we have in common. We become effective messengers in a saving solidarity of justice, peace, unity. And the more we commit ourselves to this vision, the more truthfully and joyfully will we celebrate the Eucharist as the sacrament of unity.[19]

Häring goes on to say that before we can celebrate the Eucharist as an effective sign of unity, we need a "manifold conversion and reconciliation." By this he means reconciling ourselves not only with the true meaning of bread, wine, and all earthly things but also with our capacities to become once again what they were meant to be: "signs of solidarity before God, the giver of all good things." This is possible only if we reconcile ourselves with God in and through the Eucharist, in gratitude so deeply felt that we truly offer all that we are and all that we have to God in the service of one another.[20]

With the larger umbrella of reconciliation now open, we turn our attention to the ritual sacrament of reconciliation, the rite of penance.

The Rite of Penance

The historical sweep covered in the last chapter brought us to the threshold of the Second Vatican Council. The bishops at the Second Vatican Council, recognizing the reality that being reconciled with God and the Christian community is a cause for great rejoicing and not humiliation, noticed a basic inconsistency between that reality and the way in which reconciliation was accomplished—in the dark, in secrecy, with anonymity. In the Constitution on the Sacred Liturgy, the Council decreed that "the rite and formulas of Penance are to be revised so that they more clearly express both the nature and effect of the sacrament."[21]

It took two commissions seven years of research and discussions and more than a dozen draft documents to implement that simple statement made in the Second Vatican Council's Constitution on the Sacred Liturgy. Their work began with an attempt to determine difficulties inherent in present practice. Questionnaires completed in France, England, Scotland, the United States, Australia, and Africa were analyzed. The writings of numerous scholars were collected and studied as well. All the research indicated "a growing dissatisfaction with the sacrament of penance as well as a desire to restore vitality to it by means of a less mechanical and formal practice that would bring out more clearly the social and communal aspect of both sin and reconciliation."[22] A communal ritual to complement the individual ritual was also cited as a desire.

Throughout the process the commissions maintained the focus that "sin is by its nature both an offense against God and a wound inflicted on the Church; sacramental reconciliation is reconciliation with both God and the Church; and the entire Christian community works together for the conversion of sinners."[23]

In 1973, at long last, Pope Paul VI approved the *Ordo Paenitentiae (Rite of Penance),* which gives a better expression of celebrating that reconciliation between God and the sinner and is more consistent with the way the community prays in common today. In the *Praenotanda*, or pastoral introduction, we are given an overview of the reform in six sections. The text begins with situating the "mystery" of reconciliation in the history of salvation. "The Father has shown forth his mercy by reconciling the world to himself in Christ and by making peace for all things on earth and in heaven by the blood of Christ on the cross."[24] Immediately we see the two dimensions of Jesus' mission. Jesus walked the way with us, first calling us out of darkness and then into his wonderful light. He not only preached repentance but also welcomed sinners.

Similarly, this pastoral introduction also emphasizes two dimensions: our immersion into the "mystery" of reconciliation first through baptism and only later through the sacrament of penance. Quoting Saint Ambrose, the first section concludes: "The Church possesses both water and tears; the water of baptism, the tears of penance."[25] This provides a smooth transition into the second section of the introduction, which discusses the reconciliation of penitents in the life of the Church.

Of its very nature, as the ongoing presence of Christ on earth, the Church is holy. However, by including sinners within its company, in addition to being holy it is at the same time always in need of purification. As Church we seek this continual repentance in many different ways: by enduring our own difficulties, carrying out works of mercy and charity, and adopting ever more fully the outlook of the gospel message. In this way the people of God stand before the world as a sign of conversion expressed in their lives and celebrated in the liturgy.[26] This section continues with a description of the nature of contrition, confession, satisfaction, and absolution, and the importance of frequent confession.

The third section of the introduction describes the offices and ministries in the reconciliation of penitents, beginning with a description of the role of the Christian community in the celebration of penance and a discussion of the dispositions required in the ministers of reconciliation and the penitents.

The celebrations themselves are discussed next in the pastoral introduction, followed by two concluding sections on penitential celebrations and adaptations.

Celebrating Reconciliation

The *Rite of Penance* consists of three different forms that the celebration may take: one individual form and two communal forms. The *Praenotanda* makes no reference to one preferred form, although the first form is more familiar to us. "Just as the wounds of sin are varied and multiple in the life of individuals and of the community," the rite states, "so too the healing that penance provides is varied."[27]

All three forms have the same common elements but differ in size and shape, we might say. We will look at some of the common elements in isolation before describing each form of the rite.

The **proclamation of the word of God**, or a reading from Scripture, is an important element of each form of the rite, for it is "through the word of God Christians receive light to recognize their sins and are called to conversion and to confidence in God's mercy."[28]

Confession of sins, "which comes from true knowledge of self before God and from contrition for those sins,"[29] is a second common element of the rite. The confession follows the penitent's examination of his or her own conscience and presumes the penitent's openness to God's grace through the spiritual ministry of the priest.

A third common element is **prayer**, beginning with the prayer of both priest and penitent before approaching the sacrament. "The priest should call upon the Holy Spirit so that he may receive enlightenment and charity,"[30] and the penitent should pray to God for forgiveness. Within the context of the rite there are several other moments of prayer, concluding of course with the prayer of absolution:

> God, the Father of mercies,
> through the death and resurrection of his Son
> has reconciled the world to himself
> and sent the Holy Spirit among us
> for the forgiveness of sins;
> through the ministry of the Church
> may God give you pardon and peace,
> and I absolve you from your sins
> in the name of the Father, and of the Son,
> and of the Holy Spirit.[31]

Reconciliation of Individual Penitents

As mentioned earlier, the *Rite of Penance* presumes that both priest and penitent have prepared to celebrate this sacrament: the priest by praying to the Holy Spirit for enlightenment and charity; the penitent by comparing his or her life to the gospel and praying to God for forgiveness.[32] Only then do they begin the ritual celebration of the sacrament of reconciliation properly.

The ritual instructs the priest to welcome the penitent warmly and to greet him or her with kindness, which would appear to presume some informal exchange of words before beginning to pray. There is no one way to begin the ritual, which can be disconcerting for those of us who were rigidly trained to snap to attention as soon as the slide in the confessional box opened, and to sputter out, as quickly as possible, "Bless me, Father, for I have sinned it is two weeks since my last confession I accuse myself of . . ."

While the penitent makes the sign of the cross (which the priest may also do), the priest invites the penitent to trust in God. The priest may use his own words for this or one of several texts found in the ritual.[33]

The place of Scripture in the celebration of this sacrament is somewhat tenuous. Although the ritual states that the reading of the word of God is "optional," it presumes that if a text of Holy Scripture is not read at this point in the ritual, it did form part of the preparation.[34] Scripture is hardly optional, because "through the word of God Christians receive light to recognize their sins and are called to conversion and to confidence in God's mercy."[35]

Usually there is some specific Scripture text that has spurred me to reexamine my spiritual life and its various detours, and to return to the "straight path" mapped out by Jesus in the gospel. Where that is true, it would be appropriate for the penitent to bring that text into the celebration of the sacrament. Otherwise, the confessor makes an appropriate selection.

It was a topsy-turvy time in my life. At the time I referred to it as my "midlife crisis," although I now see that it was but the first of several such turning points that shaped who I am today. In the midst of it I saw God urging me in a different direction. I found myself haunted by the God Francis Thompson described in the poem "The Hound of Heaven."[36] Like Thompson, I felt more fugitive than faithful, and in time wanted to confess that sinfulness and celebrate reconciliation with God and the Church.

By that time I had also come to yearn for good sacramental celebrations. Unsatisfied by "quickies" generally practiced in the local parish, I gave thoughtful consideration to the person with whom I would celebrate this sacrament. One priest came to mind, not only because he was a good celebrant but also because I knew that my life had followed a path similar to his. He agreed to celebrate the sacrament with me one Sunday afternoon before Vespers.

He came vested in alb and stole, which was my first surprise. I couldn't remember any other celebrant dressing for the occasion before. We began the ritual. He had selected a Scripture text for the occasion that perfectly addressed my spiritual state at the moment. Jim knew where I was because he had once been there himself. Fellow prodigals met together on the road, and like those other two pilgrims on the road to Emmaus, we welcomed the third to our company.

Others have celebrated the sacrament of reconciliation with me since, but that celebration remains paradigmatic for me. Now Jim has gone on to know that greater reconciliation that lies beyond this life, but he left me a legacy that continues to shape my spirituality and ministry. "The reconciliation celebrated in the sacrament of penance is first and foremost a reconciliation with oneself, which becomes the sign of reconciliation with God."[37]

For something the ritual deems "optional," it provides an unusual number of alternate texts[38] and goes on to state that the priest and penitent may choose other readings from Scripture beside those alternate texts suggested. Remembering that the ritual was developed twenty years ago, before the Scriptures had returned to a central place in the life of ordinary Catholics, perhaps it is less surprising that the ritual seems to put reading the word of God in a secondary place. Still, the text placed first in the *editio typica*[39] is of particular significance.

The instruction is to look to Jesus, "who suffered to save us and rose again for our justification,"[40] rooting this sacramental celebration firmly in the paschal mystery. The first pericope that follows is taken from Isaiah 53:4-6:

> Surely he has borne our infirmities
>   and carried our diseases;
> yet we accounted him stricken,
>   struck down by God and afflicted.
> But he was wounded for our transgressions,
>   crushed for our iniquities
> upon him was the punishment that made us whole,
>   and by his bruises we are healed.
> All we like sheep have gone astray;
>   we have all turned to our own way . . .
>
> (Isa 53:4-6)

This becomes the immediate context for the penitent to confess his or her sins, perhaps beginning with the more general formula "I confess to almighty God. . . ." The rite does not presume that this is the penitent's monologue but that the priest provides appropriate spiritual counsel and encouragement. The priest also proposes an act of penance, which the penitent accepts. Ideally, these acts of penance relate to the liturgical cycle as well as to the needs of penitents in helping them to renew their lives. The penitent accepts the act of penance, is asked to make a simple act of contrition,[41] and receives absolution from God through the ministry of the priest. Together they praise the mercy of God and give thanks in a short invocation taken from Scripture, such as:

> *Priest:* Give thanks for God is good.
>
> *Penitent:* God's mercy endures forever.

The priest then dismisses the penitent, who has been reconciled with these or similar words:

> Go in peace,
> and proclaim to the world
> the wonderful works of God
> who has brought you salvation.[42]

Thus the penitent, by experiencing and proclaiming the mercy of God in his or her life, celebrates *with* the priest the liturgy by which the Church continually renews itself.[43]

Celebrations of Mercy

Communal celebrations, as the rite indicates, show more clearly the ecclesial nature of penance and are more consistent with the concept of Church understood by the Second Vatican Council.[44] The second and third forms of the rite of penance are both communal celebrations. They both begin with a liturgy of the Word and, following a brief homily, include some form of communal examination of conscience. The second form provides an opportunity for penitents to confess their sins individually to the priest and receive absolution. The third form, used when there are not sufficient confessors available to hear individual confessions properly within a suitable period of time,[45] provides for "common absolution" rather than individual absolution. The communal forms then conclude with the community praising and giving thanks for God's mercy, usually in song.

Pastoral practice has demonstrated that celebrations of this sacrament are not a matter of either/or, but of both/and. As will be discussed at greater length in the following chapter, there are times in the liturgical cycle when communal celebrations are most appropriate. Communal celebrations in preparation for the reception of First Eucharist and confirmation are also important because they draw the extended community into the sacramental moment.

For several years at the university I served as a catechist for children in the Sunday community who were preparing to receive the sacrament of reconciliation for the first time. Rather than have a separate service for them, it was decided that they would receive the sacrament at the community's regularly scheduled communal celebration during the Lenten season.

The chapel was crowded with adults and five or six squeaky-clean, highly polished children, all dressed up for this wonderful celebration of God's mercy. I had not told them how to dress, but they looked as though they were headed for a birthday party. That was their understanding of the nature of the celebration.

They sat with their families during the service. When the time for individual confessions came, they let a few adults pave the way, but the children's approach to the sacrament was contagious. During the service several adults came to me to say that they had not received the sacrament in ten or twenty years but felt moved to follow the children. Of course, the text from Isaiah, "and a little child shall lead them," came to mind.

This is the Church: the young and old, the hale and halt, the robust and weary—sinners all, in need of God's tender embrace. Where communal celebrations also include the priests confessing their sins to one another, this reality is most clear.

Ambassadors of Reconciliation

At the beginning of this discussion of reconciliation, we recalled the words of Saint Paul in the Letter to the Corinthians, where he named us ambassadors of reconciliation. That theme echoes again in the words of the *Rite of Penance:*

> The whole Church, as a priestly people, acts in different ways in the work of reconciliation that has been entrusted to it by the Lord. Not only does the Church call sinners to repentance by preaching the word of God, but it also intercedes for them and helps penitents with maternal care and solicitude to acknowledge and confess their sins and to obtain the mercy of God, who alone can forgive sins. Further, the Church becomes itself the instrument of the conversion and absolution of the penitent through the ministry entrusted by Christ to the apostles and their successors.[46]

The responsibility of the Christian community, therefore, is to continue this ministry of reconciliation by interceding for sinners until we experience the ultimate reconciliation in the kingdom of God promised in the Book of Revelation:

> See, the home of God is among mortals.
> He will dwell with them as their God;

they will be his people
and God himself will be with them;
he will wipe every tear from their eyes.
Death will be no more,
for the first things have passed away (Rev 21:3-5).

Conclusion

As was stressed early in this chapter, sacramental theology
is developmental, and consequently one thing we can be sure
of is that our understanding of sacramental reconciliation tomorrow will not be as it is today. Peter Fink sees that we are
"caught between an old sacramental consciousness that has
not yet disappeared and a new sacramental consciousness that
is only in the early stages of gestation."[47] I sometimes wonder
what the new consciousness will look like and will share some
of my explorations and theorization in the concluding chapter.

Notes

1. Mary Collins, "Culture and Forgiveness," in *Worship: Renewal
to Practice* (Washington, D.C.: Pastoral Press, 1987) 38. See also Larry
Powell, *Hunger of the Heart: Communion at the Wall* (Dubuque, Ia.:
Islewest Publishers, 1995).

2. John Thomas, *Coventry Cathedral* (London: Unwin Hyman,
1987) 68–69.

3. For fear of vandalism, the original cross was placed in St.
Michael's Hall in the undercroft of the new cathedral. A replica now
stands in its place in the ruins.

4. See Karl Rahner, "Questions on the Theology of Sacraments,"
Theological Investigations, vol. 23 (New York: Crossroad, 1992) 189–
194.

5. For a thorough discussion, see Bernard Leeming, S.J., *The Prin-
ciples of Sacramental Theology* (London: Longman, Green and Co.,
1956) 553–589.

6. *The Catechism of the Catholic Church* [CCC], no. 405.

7. Ibid.

8. Christopher Kiesling, "Infant Baptism," *Worship* 42 (1968) 621.

9. *Rite of Christian Initiation of Adults* [RCIA], no. 141.

10. RCIA, no. 143.

11. RCIA, no. 154a.

12. RCIA, no. 168a.

13. RCIA, no. 175a.

14. See *This Is the Night* (Chicago: Liturgy Training Publications, 1992).

15. See Nathan Mitchell, "The Table of Eucharist: Christian Fellowship and Christian Forgiveness," *Rite of Penance: Commentaries,* ed. Nathan Mitchell (Washington, D.C.: Liturgical Conference, 1978) 3:62-81.

16. See Annibale Bugnini, *The Reform of the Liturgy 1948–1975* (Collegeville, Minn.: The Liturgical Press, 1990) 477–482.

17. *Documents on the Liturgy 1963–1979* [DOL], no. 1996. The direction that episcopal conferences select only one of the prayers was never enforced and apparently was later abandoned.

18. *Notitiae* 13 (1977) 555–556; 17 (1981) 23.

19. Bernard Häring, *The Eucharist and Our Everyday Life* (New York: Seabury, 1979) 52.

20. Ibid., 53.

21. Constitution on the Sacred Liturgy, no. 72.

22. Bugnini, *The Reform of the Liturgy,* 664–665. For a thorough discussion of the various stages, documents, and difficulties encountered in this process, see pp. 664–683.

23. Ibid., 665.

24. *Rite of Penance* [RP], no. 1.

25. Letter 41:12; PL 16:1116.

26. RP, nos. 3–4.

27. RP, no. 7.

28. RP, no 17.

29. RP, no. 6b.

30. RP, no. 15.

31. RP, no. 46.

32. RP, no. 15.

33. RP, no. 42.

34. The Irish ritual, by contrast, does not make the reading from Scripture "optional."

35. RP, no. 17.

36. See Francis Thompson, *Complete Poetical Works of Francis Thompson* (New York: Boni and Liveright, 1913).

37. Christian Duquoc, "Real Reconciliation and Sacramental Reconciliation," in *Sacramental Reconciliation,* Concilium 61, ed. Edward Schillebeeckx (New York: Herder & Herder, 1971) 36.

38. Eleven texts are listed in no. 43 of the ritual, with a hundred suggested alternates in the appendix.

39. RP, no. 72.

40. Ibid.

41. The ritual offers several suggestions of texts, but unless the penitent has access to them they go unused.

42. RP, no. 47.

43. RP, no. 11.

44. RP, no. 22.

45. RP, no. 31.

46. RP, no. 8.

47. Peter E. Fink, S.J., *Praying the Sacraments* (Washington, D.C.: Pastoral Press, 1991) 95.

Chapter 6

For the Sake of the World:
Reclaiming Reconciliation

Rather than sit back, form committees, or issue pastoral letters hoping to hang on to some vestige of the Roman Catholic practice of confession we recall from the 1950s, reclaiming reconciliation for our time requires us to go beneath the surface of religious practice to the myth level that supports practice. A way to begin this descent to the myth level is to address the key question anthropologist Margaret Mead posed:

> How can we give people rituals that will carry them through crises, rituals that will enable each individual, however deep his grief or confusion, however high his excitement, to reach out to the feelings of others who have experienced the same thing, and to his own previous experiences, and to reach out in a way that gives depth and meaning to the present?[1]

The former Soviet Union addressed itself seriously to that very question in 1953 when people were still turning to traditional Church rituals, despite reprisals, at significant moments in their lives. A Conference on Socialist Rituals was held in May 1964, inaugurating special days to honor various occupations, but this still did not satisfy the people's basic need for ritual. Further attempts to incorporate the symbols and traditions of Holy Russia into everyday Soviet life were still unsatisfactory. Finally, in 1983 the Ukraine developed elaborate socialist rites for life's thresholds: birth, marriage, and death. The development of such rites was "part of a Soviet effort to transfer to the state some of the symbolic and ceremonial functions of the church."[2]

The issue is not frivolous, for ritual is not tangential to human life. Ritual touches the core of our humanity, and as scholars conclude, ritual even has a biogenetic basis. The reason for this, they point out, is that ritual deals with basic human problems—with the need to overcome the radical and dangerous polarity of existence to which all myths call attention. Ritual also provides for the human need to unite contingent, vulnerable human beings with some Power that is ultimate, omnipotent, and deathless. Biogeneticists go even further; they contend that the myth-making and ritual-resolving capacities of human beings have a neurological basis. Human religious ritual is not simply a product of culture but is rooted in the evolution of the central nervous system. They argue that this propensity is "hardwired" into us as humans.[3]

Often myths are regarded as fanciful stories that entertain children, but the reality is that a culture's myths are *formational* rather than *informational*. They are a recapitulation or "instant replay" of the whole evolutionary history that has made us who we are. Rollo May has written that "myths are essential to the process of keeping our souls alive and bringing us new meaning in a difficult and often meaningless world."[4] They carry the values of the society and enable us to understand our place in that society. Of themselves, myths unite and often reconcile the dualities of life: conscious and unconscious, historical and present, individual and social, which form a narration that is passed down from age to age.[5] While myths are the narration, rituals are their physical expressions—the myth in bodily form, so to speak. Together, rituals and myths supply fixed points in a world of bewildering change and disappointment.[6]

The fixed point supplied by the Church's ritual of reconciliation is that no matter what the sinner has done, there is forgiveness waiting in God's healing embrace and a place waiting at the Eucharistic table. We saw in our brief excursion through history in Chapter Four that the myth-level gradually began to be obscured by layers of legalism. Those layers moved the believing community further and further from the simple words of Jesus: "If you forgive others their trespasses, your heavenly

Father will also forgive you; but if you do not forgive others, neither will your Father forgive your trespasses" (Matt 6:14-15).

The essence of being reconciled, of restoring the unity of the Body of Christ, was similarly obscured as vision kept narrowing down to the minute failures of individuals.

> During his public life Jesus not only forgave sins, but also made plain the effect of this forgiveness: he reintegrated forgiven sinners into the community of the People of God from which sin had alienated or even excluded them. A remarkable sign of this is the fact that Jesus receives sinners at his table, a gesture that expresses in an astonishing way both God's forgiveness and the return to the bosom of the people of God."[7]

How far we had been distanced from this experience!

The Way It Is

In addressing himself to the future of reconciliation in the Church, Bishop Patrick R. Cooney of Gaylord, Michigan, made some observations regarding the state of the sacrament from his perspective as priest, pastor, and bishop. As you read through them, you will see reason for hope as well as cause for concern. In all, his observations confirm those made in the beginning of this book:

1. The faithful do not celebrate the individual rite of reconciliation frequently.

2. The rite for communal celebration with individual confession and absolution has almost disappeared, and where it has not, it has simply become a communal preparation for the individual rite.

3. Although the rite of communal celebration of reconciliation with general absolution is celebrated infrequently, where it has been celebrated there is intense spiritual involvement.

4. The rite of reconciliation of individual penitents as fully outlined in the ritual books is more often replaced by a

brief form, in most cases the preconciliar rite with a changed absolution prayer.

5. Tension remains regarding the implementation of first confession prior to first communion.

6. "Devotional confession" is an area of concern.

7. The Rite for the Communal Celebration of Reconciliation with Individual Confession and Absolution is awkward and unwieldy when the congregation is large.

8. The Rite for the Communal Celebration of Reconciliation with General Absolution is still surrounded by tension and is likely to become more restricted in the future.[8]

Bishop Cooney's synthesis, as well as the discussion provided in the preceding chapters, makes it clear that we do not have a crisis in theology but in mystagogy.

Moving to Mystagogy

When the rites of Christian initiation were revised in the 1970s, I feared two things: that translators would find a more relevant word than "mystagogy" and that the last stage in the process would be eclipsed entirely. While we have survived the first hurdle and the word "mystagogy" remains in our texts if not in our hearts, I am not so sure that we yet understand the spiritual significance of the last stage. Mystagogy is far beyond the pale of our cultural horizon and is moving even farther away at a lightning pace.

Liturgically, the term mystagogy is used to refer to the time immediately following the reception of the sacraments of initiation. In the early Church this was the time when the newly initiated first learned about the mysteries of the faith. They received Eucharist before learning how the community understood and explained the transformation of the elements. They had all their sins washed away in the waters of baptism before they learned to analyze sin and its impact on the community.[9]

Today most of the mysteries of the faith are explained quite exhaustively during the time of the catechumenate, and we retain only the terminology of mystagogy. Elsewhere I have described it as similar to a honeymoon for the new members of the community.[10] More regular practice of reflecting on the mysteries of faith in general would surely enliven preaching in the community, enable us to live more balanced lives, to celebrate our beliefs more robustly, and to hand on the faith to our children and our children's children.

In all the books and articles on the subject of sacramental reconciliation I have read in the last thirty years (and my reading has been extensive), no priest has ever described his experience of being a sinner and experiencing sacramental reconciliation himself. Even at an international ecumenical symposium focused specifically on the sacrament of penance, not one cleric in our English-speaking discussion group referred to his or her personal experience of being reconciled. In all such discussions, however, that is the bottom line: we are all sinners.

That observation has led me to invite a guest speaker into my course on forgiveness and reconciliation whenever and wherever I teach it. I usually invite one of my priest-colleagues, but I remind him that he must join the conversation as a sinner as well as a confessor. As a result, we have had some extraordinary classes in which everyone walked away with a deeper experience of God's merciful embrace. The model works for Alcoholics Anonymous. Why should we not expect it to work for us sinners who stand in need of God's mercy?

Living on the edge of the third millennium, we have come to expect easy answers and quick solutions to questions and problems we barely have time to frame. Technology is moving at such a numbing pace that before we can even master the latest piece of electronic equipment, it is obsolete. Often it seems that people do not want to be engaged by mystery but entertained in spite of it.

There are life experiences, however, that plunge us into mystery with a suddenness that we are unable to escape. Once amiable rivers turn tyrant, the child next door is abducted and brutally murdered, fires burn out of control, swallowing up not only homes and lives but nature's protective sheathing as well, and we stand speechless. Such is the time for mystagogy.

Although he might not have known it at the time, T. S. Eliot was speaking of mystagogy when he wrote in "The Dry Salvages":

> We had the experience but missed the meaning
> and approach to the meaning restores the experience
> in a different form. . . .[11]

Challenged by the Culture

Once upon a time America was more than a place, James Lincoln Collier reminded us in his book *The Rise of Selfishness in America:* "It was an idea, an idea so powerful that it inflamed the imaginations of men and women around the world and led them everywhere to topple emperors and kings. Many would argue that the world no longer admires the United States of America. It envies our prosperity and our freedoms, but it does not admire us. Yes, immigrants continue to swarm in, but mainly for the abundance of things that we have. They do not come because of an idea. And Liberty weeps to see what we have done with her gift."[12]

I began my college education as a chemistry major, and I recall making various types of solutions. In a supersaturated solution, there is too much solid matter to be absorbed by the solution, and consequently some of the solid material is lost from the solution and settles at the bottom of the beaker. Ours is a supersaturated society. We have too much of almost everything—noise, information, consumer goods. My concern, both as a theologian and as an educator, is that what will be lost in this supersaturated society is what we need most to survive as a people: the essence of our humanity, our souls.

Mystagogy requires leisure, and if one is totally absorbed with other concerns, one never has leisure necessary to focus on God alone.[13] To quote the poet William Wordsworth, "for this, for everything we are out of tune. It moves us not."

In substantiating his diagnosis that we Americans are "amusing ourselves to death," Neil Postman observed that all public discourse—politics, religion, news, athletics, education, and commerce—has gradually taken on the form of entertainment, "transformed into congenial adjuncts of show business." Those who have sold their souls, even inadvertently, to the entertainment industry will always have unrealistic expectations about liturgy. The complaint "I don't get anything out of the liturgy" can simply be translated as "It isn't entertaining enough."

One sees that immediately on the evening news on commercial television. Little of real substance is ever presented these days, and what little one does find is never developed. We are fed sound bites of significance and pseudo-significance, titillated but not informed.

Defined as "a performance intended to amuse or divert," entertainment is the exact opposite of ritual prayer, which is intended to focus and redirect us. No wonder there is so much personal disillusionment with the liturgy: it puts too many demands on us in a world that increasingly requires less and less. We expect upbeat music, relevant homilies, and a service that makes us feel good.

Who has room for God?

Who comes to the Eucharist with an emptiness that only God can fill?

Who comes in humility to the Church to seek forgiveness for sin when sin is what tantalizes us on the big screen?

Once upon a time people used to fast before coming to worship. By the time this spiritual discipline had passed out of our experience in the mid 1960s, however, it had devolved into a meaningless exercise in clockwatching. Although I am not recommending a return to such often "mindless" practices, there is something to be said for coming to the banquet table hungry—not just fasting from food but hungering both physically and spiritually. Physical hunger that reminds us ultimately of our deep spiritual hunger for communion with one another and with God can be a powerful religious experience.

Gathered Around the Table

The Eucharistic table is the place to bring both life's struggles and questions and to celebrate the mystery—the mystery that death becomes life—the mystery that "abides and draws everything toward life."[14] Around the table gathers the company of believers, sinners all. They include believers not just of our time but from two thousand years of believing. During wars and pestilence, floods and droughts, the young and the feeble come dancing or limping to take their place in our circle of faith. This action "makes the Church present and manifests her as the visible sign of the communion in Christ between God and men." Around that table the faithful are caught up in the new life of the community, a life that "involves the 'conscious, active, and fruitful participation' of everyone"[15]—accent on "everyone."

I think the point that Jesus tried to make so graphically was that this act of "remembering and giving thanks" that we call Eucharist is not just about the past; it is also about the present and even more importantly about the future. Jesus did not intend for us simply to remember his oblation but to be oblations ourselves and to spend our lives in service of one another. It is as if Jesus is still urging us down through the centuries, "Make your Eucharistic table a piece of lavish abundance and extravagant service, where the tired, the poor, the hungry, and all who, driven by despair and need, may find real food, real rest, real comfort, real nurture."[16] Do this!

"To participate in the meal is to enact that vision, to surrender oneself to its value, meaning and truth," Nathan Mitchell writes. In coming to the Eucharistic meal, we testify to our common belief that it is the Lord Jesus who sustains and nourishes us, and we pledge that we will likewise sustain and nourish one another with the bread that is our lives. That is our pledge to humanity. Speaking in Philadelphia in 1976, Fr. Pedro Arrupe, S.J., reminded us that "if there is hunger anywhere in the world, then our celebration of the Eucharist is somehow incomplete everywhere in the world."[17]

Father Eugene LaVerdiere, S.S.S., elaborates on this concept in his book *Dining in the Kingdom of God*. He approaches Eucharist by examining ten meals that Jesus ate with others as described in the Gospel according to Luke, giving us the demands of Eucharist, you could say. LaVerdiere summarizes seven challenges of table solidarity that we could each spend a lot of time reflecting on in our own lives. He says that those who dine with Jesus "must be willing to be transformed by his presence . . . to reach out in loving reconciliation . . . be ready for the unexpected . . . listen attentively to the word of the Lord . . . attend to interior cleanness . . . seek the lowest place, and the host must invite the poor and helpless and offer their own lives that others might live."[18]

Both the latest *Catechism of the Catholic Church* and the Church's most ancient tradition repeatedly refer to the "mystery" of faith. That is a term we must all begin to focus on more. Many of our "absent brethren" think that they can't come to the table unless they have all the answers and give complete assent to every papal and episcopal utterance. When we put the accent on "mystery," however, we begin to see the banqueting table in better focus.

Regardless of what we may have done along the way, it is so important to keep on coming back to the table, to keep both memory and hope alive. The *Catechism of the Catholic Church* reminds us that the entire assembly "should prepare itself to encounter its Lord and to become 'a people well disposed.'"[19] This "preparation of hearts" it recognizes to be the joint work of the Holy Spirit and the assembly.

Too often we discuss Eucharist almost exclusively in terms of what happens to the bread and wine, how relevant the homily is, whether or not the prayers are inclusive or the celebrant dynamic. The first Christians focused instead on what happened to the people who share bread and wine in memory of Christ. We have two thousand years of stories about people whose lives have been transformed by their experiences around the Christian family table. Some are celebrated as saints, but others are ordinary citizens who are able to do extraordinary things because their faith in themselves, in God, and in the community has been strengthened at Eucharist. Those are the stories we must remember to tell one another.

Reclaiming Reconciliation

As if in response to the question posed by Margaret Mead at the beginning of this chapter, the bishops gathered at Vatican Council II responded. Into the darkness of those black boxes where we anonymously shed all those dreadful sins, the Council spoke:

> The rite and formulas of Penance are to be revised so that
> they more clearly express both the nature and effect of
> the sacrament.[20]

If there is anything that unites us as a human community, as
we have said before, it is our propensity to sin. Jesus came to
call sinners to himself, not the self-righteous, as we are reminded in the Gospel (Matt 9:13; Mark 2:17). Hidden away in
darkened confessionals, ashamed to be seen in our true humanity, we were far from celebrating the reconciliation we
have experienced through Jesus.

Although the Council did not address the issue of sin directly or at great length, it did encourage continued instruction:

> . . . the catechesis must impress on the minds of the
> faithful the distinctive character of penance as a detesta-
> tion of sin because it is an offense against God. The role
> of the church in penitential practices is not to be omitted,
> and the need to pray for sinners should be emphasized.[21]

There are some areas of success with the new rite of
penance, as noted earlier by Bishop Cooney, which speak very
well for an understanding of the communal effect of sin. During the seasons of Advent and Lent, increasing numbers of
parishes are celebrating the rite of penance communally.
Whether or not particular need determines the use of the second or third rite, the members of the community find in these
communal sacramental experiences a meaning that is different
from what they found in the practice of frequent individual
confession. It seems evident that if my sin affects the community, I would want to seek reconciliation with and through the
community. In this case the practice of communal penance,
where it is permitted, is indeed reflecting a theology of sin that
is fuller than that which flourished in the 1950s. Therefore,
statistics on the number of people going to confession are not
an accurate barometer for the community's understanding of
sin.[22]

The work of reclaiming reconciliation will be more successful if we plant seeds in fertile ground, like that noted above.

Testing the soil, therefore, is an important task because ahead of us still lie many years for allowing the power of the Spirit unleashed through Vatican Council II to breathe freely among us. This will draw us closer to our true identity as the people of God joined in the Mystical Body of Christ.

> The people of God believes that it is led by the Spirit of the Lord who fills the whole world. Impelled by that faith, they try to discern the true signs of God's presence and purpose in the events, the needs and the desires which it shares with the rest of humanity today. For faith casts a new light on everything and makes known the full ideal which God has set for humanity, thus guiding the mind towards solutions that are fully human.[23]

By "fertile ground" I mean pragmatic indicators of a readiness to receive the word of God. The exceptional popularity of *Les Miserables,* I believe, is one such example. Written by Victor Hugo in 1862, in recent years the musical version of the story that condemns social injustice in nineteenth-century France has played to standing-room crowds for more than a decade. I have seen the New York City production four times myself, entranced by the theme of forgiveness and greatness of soul that is at its heart. What fertile ground for preaching!

Another example can be found in the rich heritage of the Roman Catholic community. Ember Days and/or Rogation Days might be recovered and put at the service of this project of reclaiming reconciliation for the sake of the world. Instead of looking to "new age" rituals, this might be the very time we need to cast a backward glance to our own neglected heritage.

Ember Days were three days set aside for fasting, abstinence, and prayer during each of the four seasons of the year. They were the Wednesday, Friday, and Saturday after the Feast of Saint Lucy (December 13), the First Sunday of Lent, Pentecost, and the Feast of the Holy Cross on September 14. I use the past tense here because since the revision of the Roman calendar in 1969, the observance of Ember Days was left to the discretion of each nation's conference of bishops. Originating, it is presumed, in the agricultural feasts of ancient Rome, these days were observed by Christians as a time to pray for blessing during the different seasons of the year. It also gave the community an opportunity to seek God's blessing on those who would be ordained to the clergy during the Embertides. The Washington National Cathedral, for example, has reclaimed the practice and invites people to a Friday evening of prayer during Embertides. "Today many of us strive to offer our work as a living prayer to the world no matter what our profession or occupation," the notice reads. "In this present-day program of song, prayer, guided meditation and reflection, clergy and lay people together are invited to refresh themselves and renew the connection to the Holy Spirit that empowers the deep center of their lives."[24]

In Conclusion

This book opened with a reference to the cavernous silence into which Terry Anderson spoke upon being released from seven years of torture and imprisonment as a hostage in Lebanon. Let me end by returning again to his reflection on that experience—an exquisite example of mystagogy. *Den of Lions,* Anderson's memoir of those years, should be required reading for all Christians. Not a catalogue of horrors that fixates on man's inhumanity to man, it is a story of how the human spirit, sustained by faith, hope, and love, can not only endure, but triumph.

For those not familiar with his background as a journalist, Terry Anderson was a correspondent for the Associated Press, stationed in the Middle East. As you will soon read in his own words, he had long been alienated from his Catholic past, but like the Prodigal Son had recently turned in the direction of home.

On a visit to England in December 1984, Anderson found himself haunted by the local Catholic church. He "kept catching sight of the tall, sharply pointed traditional steeple. . . ." Every time he turned around, it was there. One day he finally entered the church, sat down in a pew, and stared at the altar and at the crucifix. Although Anderson says that he didn't pray, he recalled feeling "a perfect sense of being at home." After many years of denial, in that moment he came face to face with himself as a Catholic, a Christian. "Whatever I've done in the past," he writes, "that's what I am." He continues:

> The sense of relief, of some unrecognized strain being loosened, was powerful and immediate. I didn't know what I was going to do with my new knowledge, whether I could live up to the obligations and duties it would impose. I would have to work that out later. For now, just knowing was enough."[25]

On March 16, 1985, he was taken hostage.

Three months into his ordeal, Terry Anderson learned that a Catholic priest, Fr. Lawrence Jenco, was being held hostage in the same location. He pleaded with his captors to be allowed some time alone with the priest to confess his sins. Because the captors were religious men, they acceded to his request and the following scene unfolds:

> Cautiously, I raise my blindfold. Father Jenco, a white-haired man with a full beard and a gentle smile, is sitting cross-legged on David's mattress. We clasp hands. "I'm Lawrence Jenco." "Hi, Father. I'm Terry Anderson. I don't know where to start. It's been a very long time since I said confession."
>
> "It doesn't matter. Just go ahead." He nods in encouragement.

In *Den of Lions*, Anderson relates the details of his confession to Father Jenco, giving both the confessor and the reader a glimpse into his life as an agnostic and his recent conversion. Anderson goes on to explain that he was in the process of getting a divorce when he was kidnapped, taking upon himself most of the blame. "I was not a good man—chasing women, drinking. Seems like I just kind of lost my way for a while." Who of us has not had the experience of losing our way for a while?

Anderson says that their conversation went on for twenty minutes or more—twice the time the guards had agreed to. Throughout the encounter Anderson characterizes Father Jenco's responses as quiet and gentle. "Mostly, he just listens."

This was Anderson's first confession in twenty-five years—his "first formal step back to the church," as he puts it.

> I'd spent months wrestling with myself; months trying to understand where that moment in an English church six months ago was taking me; more months lying chained on a cot with nothing to do but examine myself, study the Bible and try to deal, alone, with my anger, frustration, remorse. This smiling, soft-spoken priest, also a hostage, dressed like me in white cotton shorts and T-shirt, frightened, in his own pain and anger received the full flood of my emotions, guilt, and concerns, returning warmth, love and understanding.

As their time together came to an end, Anderson says that he knelt beside Father Jenco and said simply, "Father, forgive me, for I have sinned, in word and in thought, in what I have done and what I have not done."

> He rests his right hand lightly on my head. "In the name of a gentle, loving God, you are forgiven." He pulls my head gently to his shoulder and hugs me. We sit back and look at each other. In a few moments, we hear a guard turning the lock on the door, and we pull our blindfolds down over our eyes.[26]

A time for embracing!

Notes

1. Margaret Mead, "Ritual and Social Crisis," in *Roots of Ritual,* ed. James D. Shaughnessy (Grand Rapids, Mich.: Eerdmans, 1973) 99.

2. Serge Schmemann, "New Soviet Rituals Seek to Replace Church's," *The New York Times* (March 15, 1983) A1, A9.

3. Nathan Mitchell, ed., "What Biogeneticists Are Saying About Ritual," *Liturgy Digest* 1:1 (Spring 1993) 53.

4. Rollo May, *The Cry for Myth* (New York: Norton, 1991) 20.

5. Ibid., 26.

6. Clyde Kluckhohn, "Myths and Rituals: A General Theory," *Harvard Theological Review* 35 (January 1942) 45–79.

7. CCC, no. 1443.

8. Patrick R. Cooney, "The Future of Reconciliation in the Church: Learning a New Art," in *Repentance and Reconciliation in the Church,* ed. Michael J. Henchel (Collegeville, Minn.: The Liturgical Press, 1987) 80–83.

9. For a complete treatment of this subject, see Enrico Mazza, *Mystagogy: A Theology of Liturgy in the Patristic Age* (New York: Pueblo, 1989).

10. See Julia Upton, R.S.M., *A Church for the Next Generation: Sacraments in Transition* (Collegeville, Minn.: The Liturgical Press, 1990) 37, 45–46; *Becoming a Catholic Christian: A Pilgrim's Guide to the Rite of Christian Initiation of Adults* (Washington, D.C.: Pastoral Press, 1993) 77–81.

11. T. S. Eliot, "The Dry Salvages," in *Four Quartets* (New York: Harcourt Brace Jovanovich, 1971) 39.

12. James Lincoln Collier, *The Rise of Selfishness in America* (New York: Oxford University Press, 1991) 264.

13. Neil Postman, *Amusing Ourselves to Death: Public Discourse in the Age of Show Business* (New York: Penguin, 1985) 3–4.

14. CCC, no. 1085.

15. CCC, no. 1071.

16. Nathan Mitchell, *Eucharist as Sacrament of Initiation* (Chicago: Liturgy Training Publications, 1994) 103.

17. Pedro Arrupe, S.J., "The Hunger for Bread . . . ," Address to the Forty-First International Eucharistic Congress, Philadelphia, 1976.

18. Eugene LaVerdiere, *Dining in the Kingdom of God: The Origins of the Eucharist According to Luke* (Chicago: Liturgical Training Publications, 1994).

19. CCC, no. 1098.

20. Constitution on the Sacred Liturgy, no. 72.

21. Constitution on the Sacred Liturgy, no. 109b.

22. See National Conference of Catholic Bishops, *Reflections on the Sacrament of Penance in Catholic Life Today: A Study Document* (Washington, D.C.: NCCB, 1990).

23. Pastoral Constitution on the Church in the Modern World, no. 11.

24. http://www.cathedral.org/cathedral/events/Ember.html. Another ancient custom was the celebration of the Rogation Days, which were prescribed days of prayer and penance in spring. There were two sets of these days (April 25, the Feast of St. Mark, and the Minor Rogation on the last three days before the Feast of the Ascen-

sion) set aside to pray for protection and invoke God's blessing on the harvest. Because they occur so close to Easter, however, they might not be as valuable for our purposes.

25. Terry A. Anderson, *Den of Lions: Memoirs of Seven Years* (New York: Crown, 1993) 58.

26. Ibid., 97–98.

Index